101 Great Gifts From Kids
Fabulous Gifts Every Child Can Make

101 GREAT Gifts

From Kids

Fabulous Gifts Every Child Can Make

Stephanie R. Mueller and Ann E. Wheeler

gryphon house®, inc.

Beltsville, MD

Dedication

From Stephanie

Thank you to my parents, and to my fellow educators who inspired and encouraged my creative side

To my husband Michael, who is so patient and supportive

To my daughter Elsa, a gift herself, who experimented along with me

From Ann

To Tony and Nick, thank you for your love and support

To Ellie Newby and the staff of Kirk of the Hills preschool, past and present, thank you for being such wonderful teachers, role models and friends

Acknowledgments

From both Stephanie and Ann

Author photos provided by Freddy Cepeda/ASC Photography

Copyright © 2002 Stephanie Mueller and Ann Wheeler

Published by Gryphon House, Inc.

10726 Tucker Street, Beltsville MD 20705

World Wide Web: http://www.gryphonhouse.com

Illustrations: Mary Rojas

Library of Congress Cataloging-in-Publication Data
Mueller, Stephanie.
    101 great gifts from kids / Stephanie Meuller and Ann Wheeler.
        p. cm.
    ISBN 0-87659-279-5
    1. Handicraft. 2. Gifts. 3. Creative activities and seat work. I. Title: One hundred and one great gifts from kids. II. Title: One hundred one great gifts from kids. III. Wheeler, Ann. IV. Title.

TT157 .M774 2002
745.5-dc21   2002019389

Bulk purchase

Gryphon House books are available at special discount when purchased in bulk for special premiums and sales promotions as well as for fund-raising use. Special editions or book excerpts also can be created to specification. For details, contact the Director of Sales at the address on the right.

Disclaimer

The publisher and the authors cannot be held responsible for injury, mishap, or damages incurred during the use of or because of the activities in this book. The authors recommend appropriate and reasonable supervision at all times based on the age and capability of each child.

Table of Contents

Chapter 6—Decorations to Display

Chapter 7—Say It with a Card

Chapter 8—Wrap It Up!

Introduction

When young children make something unique to give as a special gift for a loved one, they feel proud and successful about what they can do and share. Often these child-made gifts are treasured for years to come. With the appropriate materials, the freedom to be creative, and a little guidance, the possibilities for child-made gifts are infinite.

101 Great Gifts from Kids is full of gift-making activities for children from ages three to eight. The ideas can be used with a group of children or with one child. Most of the ideas can be created from easy-to-find household recyclables, and many of them cost only a few cents to make.

What Makes a Great Gift?

A **Great Gift**:
- is unique to the child—created without adult-imposed patterns or standards, so no two are alike.
- is open to imagination and creativity—the child's ideas, choices, and personality are integrated.
- is "owned" by the child—the child made it, investing thought, time, and energy; therefore, it means more when given to someone else.
- is made with minimal adult help—the adult selects and sets up appropriate materials for each activity, then observes as the child creates.

How to Use This Book

Table of Contents

The chapters are divided by characteristics unique to the materials or type of gift. This makes the book, and each activity, applicable to a wide variety of holidays and special occasions.

Activities

Materials

Most materials are readily available or easily obtained. Whenever possible, we suggest alternative ideas to offer flexibility based on the materials that may be on hand. Unless otherwise noted, the term *paint* indicates tempera paint and *glue* specifies white school glue. Always use materials that are appropriate for young children, such as non-toxic paints and markers, and child-size scissors. A list of commonly used Great Gift materials is on page 161.

Before Beginning

Some activities include a "Before Beginning" section, which indicates that some adult preparation is required before the child gets involved in the activity.

Make Your Great Gift

While adults can use the directions included in each activity to guide the gift-making process, the projects are the child's to create. We believe the process, the creative freedom, and the value of giving are more important than the physical appearance of the end product. Steps that may require adult help or supervision are marked with an asterisk.

As with any activity, take into consideration the developmental level and abilities of the individual child. All gift-making materials should be child-safe, non-toxic, and used under close adult supervision.

To prepare for all activities, cover the workspace, provide a smock to cover clothing, and select a safe place for wet projects to dry. Also, have an appropriate writing utensil handy to write the date and child's name on the gift.

Variation

Several activities can be modified to create a whole new gift-giving project.

Helpful Hints

Many activities include ideas to help children complete the projects, including time- and money-saving tips, options for materials, and alternative steps.

Seasonal Suggestions

Some activities include suggestions to make them unique to various holidays and/or special occasions. By simply changing the color of paint or type of paper used, a child-made gift can become uniquely seasonal. We also encourage readers to come up with adaptations to fit their specific needs.

Materials Index

This index provides an avenue to search for activities using primary materials as a guide.

Why We Wrote This Book

We noticed a need for this book when we tried to locate gift-making ideas appropriate for young children. In addition, the attendance at workshops we presented on this subject has been large, and the children who have made the gifts using the ideas in this book have been enthusiastic.

We have used the ideas in this book as early childhood teachers and parents. Some are new ideas using modern materials; others are traditional gifts or familiar art activities that have been modified to fit the developmental skills of young children.

Our goal is for all involved to experience the joy that can be found in giving and receiving unique child-made gifts.

Chapter 1

Fun with Photos!

Make frames, albums, and other personal gifts using children's photographs.

Easiest Ever Photo Frame

Trim a magnetic photo album page to frame a favorite photo.

Materials

magnetic photo album
   page
photo of child
tissue paper scraps,
   colored cellophane,
   stickers
magnetic tape

Before **B**eginning Cut the magnetic photo album page to size. It should be larger than the photograph with plenty of room for the photo and a border of collage material.*

Make Your Great Gift

1. Peel back the clear cover of the photo album page and position the photo on the sticky surface.
2. Arrange flat collage materials, such as tissue paper scraps, colored cellophane pieces, and stickers on the surface of the page around the photo.
3. Replace the clear page cover and firmly press it down on the photo and collage materials.
4. Place a piece of magnetic tape on the back of the frame.

Helpful Hint

■ Be sure to leave an undecorated space at the top of the frame so that the clear cover can re-adhere to the top of the page when replaced. If this area does end up being decorated, secure the cover at the top of the page with a piece of clear tape.*

Seasonal Suggestion

■ The magnetic photo album page can be cut into a holiday shape, such as a heart for Valentine's Day, or a flower for Mother's Day. Heart-shaped stickers can be one of the collage materials. For Thanksgiving, cut the photo album page into a leaf shape and add leaf-shaped foil confetti.

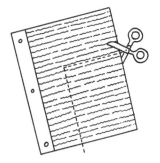

* May need adult help or supervision.

Craft Stick Picture Frame

Collage materials and glue turn these plain sticks into a fabulous frame.

Materials

craft sticks
glue
aquarium gravel, small
    pebbles, or plastic
    buttons, or plastic
    gemstones
magnetic tape

Make Your Great Gift

1. Arrange four craft sticks into a square. The ends of the craft sticks need to overlap at the corners. Glue the corners together.
2. Glue collage materials such as aquarium gravel, buttons, and plastic gemstones to the craft stick frame.
3. After the glue dries, place a strip of magnetic tape on the back of each corner of the frame.

Helpful Hints

■ Glue the craft stick frame together and allow to dry before decorating with collage materials.*
■ Adapt this gift to fit a special occasion by drawing a picture and dictating a message to the intended recipient. Secure the picture and message in the frame with clear tape.*

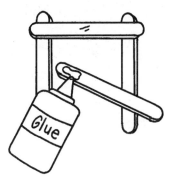

---

* May need adult help or supervision.

Fun Frame

Turn cardboard into a fabulously festive frame.

Materials

cardboard, cut to frame
   a 5" x 7" piece of
   paper*
lightweight collage
   materials, such as
   wrapping paper
   scraps, craft foam
   shapes, ribbon, and
   foil
glue
white paper, cut into
   5" x 7" rectangle*
crayons or markers
magnetic tape
tape

Make Your Great Gift

1. Decorate the cardboard frame with the lightweight collage materials.
2. While the glue dries, draw a picture for the recipient of the frame on the white paper using markers or crayons.
3. Place a strip of magnetic tape along the back of the top of the frame.
4. Put the artwork in the frame and secure it to the back of the frame with tape.

Helpful Hints

■ To create straight, even frames, use matte board that frames a 5" x 7" picture as a pattern to trace the frame shape onto the cardboard rectangle.
■ Use thin cardboard that is easily cut with scissors.

Classy Photo Frame

Enhance clear Plexiglas frames by adding buttons, sequins, and other collage materials.

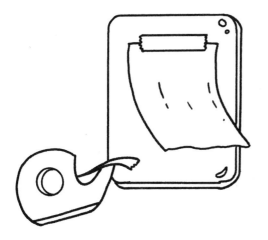

Materials

Plexiglas frames, with or
  without magnets
glue, clear drying
scrap paper
colorful buttons
sequins
tape

Before Beginning Cut a piece of scrap paper the approximate size and shape of the photo. Tape onto center of Plexiglas frame.*

Make Your Great Gift

1. Glue buttons and sequins on the Plexiglas that is not covered by the paper.
2. After the glue dries, remove the scrap paper center and insert the photo in the frame.

Helpful Hints

■ Use colored, non-toxic permanent markers instead of collage materials to create a see-through picture look or to write a simple message.
■ Use glitter glue to add sparkle to collage material border.

Seasonal Suggestion

■ Use collage materials that relate to the season or occasion. For example, add school theme stickers for a teacher gift, or blue and silver beads for Hanukkah.

* May need adult help or supervision.

Framing with Foam

Construct and decorate a photo frame using colored foam, collage materials, and magnetic tape.

Materials

colored craft foam, two colors

scissors

glue

lightweight collage material, such as beads, sequins, small foam pieces, or small buttons

magnetic tape strip, cut into pieces

photo, small

Before Beginning Trace a shape onto craft foam or to create your own shape. Cut a pair of shapes for each frame, one piece from each color of foam. Cut a smaller shape out of the middle of one of the pieces. This becomes the top of the frame.*

Make Your Great Gift

1. Glue collage materials on the outer frame piece.
2. Glue the outer frame piece to the back counterpart. Leave a slit between the two pieces at the top to slide in the photo or picture.
3. After the frame is dry, put a strip of magnetic tape on the back of the frame.
4. Use the cut-out center portion piece as a pattern for trimming the photo before it is inserted into the frame.

Helpful Hints

■ Thin craft foam works best.
■ Trace the child's hand for a personal touch and cut out the center of her palm for the photo.*

Seasonal Suggestions

■ Use simple, people shapes with a circle cut out for the photo. Decorate with wallpaper scraps, cloth scraps, ribbon, and yarn. Wonderful for Grandparents' Day, Mother's Day, and Father's Day!

* May need adult help or supervision.

Cup Photo Holder

A cup and a cardboard tube become a fancy picture display.

Materials

solid color paper party
  cup, 8 or 9 oz
cardboard wrapping
  paper tube, cut into
  a 6" section*
paint
sponge paintbrush
glue
plastic beads or jewels
photo of child

Before **B**eginning Turn the cup upside down and cut a hole in the bottom large enough for the cardboard tube to slide inside. Approximately one to two inches of the cardboard tube should be left at the bottom of the cup. Cut one-inch slits on opposite sides of the protruding end of the tube.*

Make Your Great Gift

1. Cover the cup and tube with paint, using the sponge paintbrush.
2. After the paint dries, decorate the painted cup and tube using glue and plastic beads or jewels.
3. Slide the photo into the slits at the top end of the tube. The tube should hold the picture in place, while the majority of the picture will be visible above the holder.

Seasonal Suggestion

■ Create a festive holiday photo holder by using foil shapes or gold and silver colored buttons in place of the plastic jewels. Or, use metallic paint colors of paint.

Tabletop Photo Holder

Display a precious photo in a holder made from self-hardening clay.

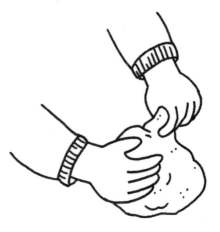

Materials

self-hardening clay,
     plain or colored
metal spatula
photo of child
thin paintbrush
tempera paint

Make Your Great Gift

1. Work a small, ball-size piece of clay into a solid, freestanding shape.
2. Use multiple colors to add designs and features to the creation. Leave a space on the top for a slit for the photo.
3. Using the metal spatula, cut a slit in the top of the holder approximately one to two inches in length. Cut deep enough so that it will hold a photo upright.*
4. After the clay dries, paint the clay holder, using a paintbrush and tempera paint.
5. Allow paint to dry. Slide the photo into the slit to complete this personal gift.

* May need adult help or supervision.

Helpful Hints

■ Cover the photo with laminate or contact paper for added durability.*

■ Using a toothpick, etch your name on the bottom of the holder before it dries.*

Seasonal Suggestions

■ Create chunky heart-shaped photo holders for Valentine's Day by forming a thick circle shape, making a dent on one edge, and pinching the clay to a point on the other to produce a heart.

■ Experiment with making assorted types of ball shapes for Father's Day. For example, create a golf ball by using white clay, rolling it into a ball, and producing indentations with an unsharpened pencil.

---

* May need adult help or supervision.

Monitor Photo Holder

Create a photo holder for a computer monitor using juice can lids and craft foam.

Materials

2 metal juice can lids

tape

self-adhesive craft
   foam, cut into
   3½" diameter circle*

scrap paper, cut in
   2" diameter circle*

glue

collage materials, such
   as craft foam pieces,
   buttons, or sequins

photo, cut in
   2" diameter circle

Before **B**eginning   Fold two juice lids at a 90° angle over the edge of a counter or other sturdy object.*

Make Your Great Gift

1. Hold the two juice lids so that two flat surfaces of the lids are back to back, forming a handle, which will sit on the monitor. The circle forms the front of the photo holder. Tape these two pieces together temporarily.
2. Pull off the paper backing from the craft foam and adhere it to the circle portion of the taped lids. The tape can be removed at this point, because the foam's adhesive backing should hold the juice lids in place.
3. Tape the two-inch paper circle in the center of the foam.
4. Glue collage materials around the border space remaining on the foam. Allow glue to dry.
5. If desired, place collage pieces on the remaining sticky foam back so that they stick out from behind.
6. Remove the paper circle and replace it with the photo cut in the same circle shape. Tape or glue into place.
7. Place the photo holder so that the "handle" portion sits on the top of a computer monitor.

Helpful Hints

■ Save on cost of materials by using poster board cut into a circle instead of craft foam. Glue it to the metal circle surface.

■ If the holder does not stay on the monitor, bend the "handle" portion a little downward.*

■ Use regular craft foam and glue it to the metal circle surface.

■ Add yarn hair, pipe cleaner arms and legs, or other items to turn this into a "person" or other creature for any occasion.

Seasonal Suggestion

■ Try other shapes, such as hearts, and attach stick-on sequins or candy hearts for a Valentine's Day gift.

"My Year" Photo Album

Display favorite memories in this photo album made of sandwich bags.

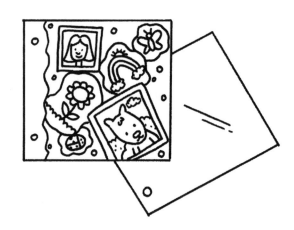

Materials

zipper-seal plastic
   sandwich bags,
   at least 5
2 thin cardboard
   squares, cut to the
   size of the sandwich
   bags*
photos of child from
   throughout the year,
   at least 10
hole punch
yarn
glue
collage materials

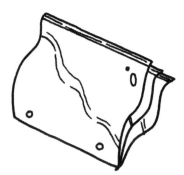

Make Your Great Gift

1. Decorate one side of each cardboard square using glue and
   collage materials.
2. While the glue is drying, look through photos from
   throughout the year. Choose 10 to use.
3. Using the hole punch make two holes along one side of
   each cardboard square, making sure that the two holes are
   about four inches apart. Then place holes in the same
   location along one side of each sandwich bag, making sure
   that the zipper seal is at the top.*
4. Place the photos inside the five sandwich bags. Position the
   photos back to back, two to a bag, so that all of the photos
   can be seen.
5. Thread yarn through holes in the sandwich bags to bind
   them together, adding a decorated square to create a front
   and back cover. Tie the yarn in a bow to hold all of the
   photo album pages firmly in place.*
6. Write your name and the date on the inside front cover of
   the album.*
7. Tie a wide ribbon around the album to add to the gift's
   appearance and help keep everything together.*

Seasonal Suggestions

- Create a winter holiday gift with collage materials such as shredded Mylar, seasonal confetti, wrapping paper scraps, and ribbon.
- Use a photo that features a fun holiday prop, such as reindeer antlers or Easter bunny ears. Trim the photo, then glue to the front of the album.*

* May need adult help or supervision.

Accordion Photo Album

Index cards are an inexpensive way to create a fun photo display.

Materials

6 photos of child
8 unruled 4" x 6" index
    cards
colored pencils
glue
clear packing tape
black marker
ribbon

Make Your Great Gift

1. Choose six photos for the photo album.
2. Use colored pencils to decorate two index cards.
3. Glue each photo to an undecorated index card.
4. Lay the eight index cards on a table with the pictures and pencil drawings face down. Place the cards so that the longer sides are touching end to end. Make sure that one decorated card is on each end of the row and the photo cards are in the middle.*
5. Use clear packing tape to secure all of the ends together on the backs of the cards. Then turn the row of index cards over and secure the front ends with tape. Fold the cards back and forth, accordion style, with the pencil drawings showing outward on the front and back cards.*
6. Write a short message or greeting to the recipient of the photo album inside the front card.*
7. Tie a ribbon around the photo album.

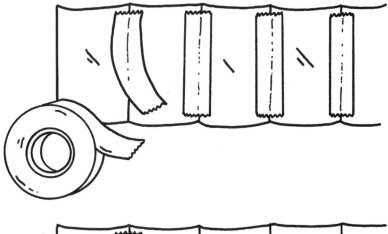

Helpful Hints

■ To protect the photo album, laminate or cover it with contact paper. Do not use heavy laminating because the cards will not fold.*

■ Write why the photo is important to you on the back of the corresponding index card.*

Seasonal Suggestion

■ Turn this photo display into a great winter holiday gift. Take pictures during each major holiday throughout the calendar year. Place all of these photos on the index cards in chronological order. Then, take a current photo of a traditional winter holiday activity, such as decorating a Christmas tree. Use this photo as the last card in the album. Use metallic color crayons to decorate the front cover card and wrap the album in metallic ribbon.

Photo Collage Box

Treasures will have a special place in this box created using a child's photo.

Materials

photo(s) of child
copy machine
scissors
small cardboard box
watered-down glue
thin paintbrush

 Before Beginning Select one or several photos. Make several black and white copies of the photo on a copy machine.*

Make Your Great Gift

1. Cut out the copies of the photo.*
2. Use watered-down glue and a thin paintbrush to glue the pictures on the box lid. Arrange the pictures so that they overlap.
3. While the lid dries, dictate a note to the recipient of the gift. Write it on a note card, and place it inside the bottom half of the box. Decorate the box bottom, too.*

Helpful Hints

■ The cardboard box used for this project must be thick and sturdy. Cardboard jewelry boxes, checkbook boxes, and small shoeboxes all work well.
■ Paint a thin coat of watered-down glue over the completed box to adhere any loose picture edges.
■ Many copy machines have a "photo" setting that will improve the appearance of copied photographs.

* May need adult help or supervision.

Chapter 2

A Garden of Gifts

Keep springtime alive with child-made flowers and outdoor decorations.

A Beautiful Bow-quet

Make a beautiful bouquet of flowers using colorful stick-on bows.

Materials

stick-on bows, new or
    used
green poster board, cut
    into 12" x 1" strips*
sheets of colored tissue
    paper
small stickers
ribbon

Make Your Great Gift

1. Choose several colors of bows.
2. Stick one bow near the top of each strip of green poster board to create flowers with stems. Used bows may have lost some of their stick and will need to be glued in place.
3. Decorate a sheet of tissue paper with small stickers.
4. Wrap the bow "flowers" in the decorated tissue paper and tie a ribbon around the tissue to secure the bouquet.*

Helpful Hints

■ Peel the paper backing off of the stick-on bows.
■ Buy tissue paper and bows during post-holiday sales.

Seasonal Suggestion

■ Use seasonal stickers to make this gift holiday specific. For example, heart stickers on the tissue paper would be perfect for Valentine's Day, while shamrock stickers could be used for a St. Patrick's Day bouquet. Red bows on green stems, with red and green tissue paper would make a beautiful Christmas gift.

* May need adult help or supervision.

"Sweet Treat" Flowers

Make someone's taste buds smile with these yummy flowers made from cupcake liners.

Make Your Great Gift

1. Choose several cupcake liners and decorate the liners and the green cardstock with markers.
2. Wrap each piece of candy in a foil or cellophane square.
3. Place several drops of glue in the center of each cupcake liner, then place a foil-wrapped candy in the middle of each liner.
4. When the glue is dry, create the flower stems by taping a folded green pipe cleaner to the back of each cupcake liner. Twist the ends of each pipe cleaner together to create a short, thick stem.*
5. Help the child roll the cardstock into a cone, decorated side out, and secure it with tape. Place the flowers inside the cone.

Materials

cupcake liners
green cardstock, cut into 5" x 4 ½" pieces*
markers
individually wrapped hard candy
foil or colored cellophane, cut into 3" squares
glue
clear tape
green pipe cleaners, folded in half

Variation

■ Instead of using candy, glue lightweight, colorful collage materials, such as tissue paper scraps, to the cupcake liners.

Helpful Hint

■ Purchasing individually wrapped candy will discourage tasting the creations.

Seasonal Suggestion

■ Cupcake liners with holiday patterns are available at local craft stores, party-supply stores, and supermarkets.

* May need adult help or supervision.

"Say Cheese" Flowers

Make someone smile with these cardstock flowers featuring the child's photos.

Materials

various colors of
   cardstock, cut into
   4" x 4" flower shapes*
crayons or markers
small photo of child
green pipe cleaners
clear tape
glue
cardstock, 1 full sheet

Before Beginning Cut cardstock into 4" x 4" flower shapes.*

Make Your Great Gift

1. Decorate at least three or four flower shapes with crayons or markers.
2. Choose one of the flowers and glue the photo in the center of it.
3. Tape green pipe cleaners to the backs of the flowers to create stems.*
4. Decorate a whole sheet of cardstock with crayons or markers.
5. Roll the piece of cardstock into a funnel shape, and secure with clear tape.*
6. Place the flowers inside the cardstock funnel to create a beautiful bouquet. Be sure the photo is clearly visible.

Helpful Hints

- Use a large flower-shaped cookie cutter as a pattern for creating the flower shapes.
- Instead of cardstock use index cards, poster board, or cardboard scraps for the flowers.

Variation

- To create a personalized bouquet, decorate four flowers, place the photo on one of the flowers and, in the middle of the other three, write a letter of the recipient's name. For example, write "MOM" or "DAD" or a simple greeting such as "HI."*

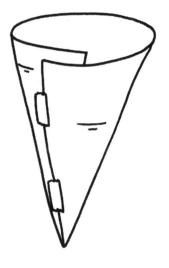

* May need adult help or supervision.

Portable Vase

A cardboard tube becomes a unique flower holder.

Materials

paper party cup,
   8 or 9 oz.
cardboard wrapping
   paper tube, cut into a
   7" section*
glue
construction paper, cut
   into 3" x 3" squares*
rubber band
paint
foam paintbrush
hole punch
yarn

Before Beginning Turn the paper cup over and cut a hole in the bottom, just large enough for the tube section to fit through. Leaving the cup upside down, slide the tube into the cup until the end of the tube is flush with the rim of the cup. Secure the tube to the cup with glue, if necessary. Close the end of the tube by wrapping a construction paper square around the hole and securing with a rubber band. This will keep the flowers from sliding through the bottom of the vase.*

Make Your Great Gift

1. Decorate the tube and base using several colors of paint and a foam paintbrush.
2. Using the hole punch, make two holes along the top edge of the tube.*
3. Tie each end of a piece of yarn to the holes in the tube to create a handle for the vase.*
4. Place fresh flowers, dried flowers, or child-made flowers inside the vase.

Seasonal Suggestions

- Use holiday paint colors to create a seasonal vase. Metallic paint colors make a festive winter holiday gift.
- Add seasonal collage materials or stickers can also be added once the paint is dry.

* May need adult help or supervision.

A Sticky Flower Arrangement

Floral stickers turn craft sticks and a plastic pot into a sensational centerpiece.

Materials

small plastic flowerpot
Styrofoam piece that
    fits inside the
    flowerpot
flower stickers
craft sticks
seasonal wire garland

Make Your Great Gift

1. Place the Styrofoam inside the flowerpot.
2. Use flower stickers to decorate the outside of the pot.
3. Place a flower sticker on one end of each craft stick.
4. Stick the plain end of each craft stick into the Styrofoam inside the flowerpot to create a flower arrangement.
5. Use seasonal wire garland to wind between the craft stick flowers.

Variation

■ Instead of placing stickers on the ends of the craft sticks, glue paper flowers to the sticks. Use markers or collage materials to decorate the flowers.

Seasonal Suggestions

■ Create a Valentine's Day arrangement by using heart stickers and paper heart shapes. For a winter holiday, use shiny star or bell stickers.
■ Use a non-toxic permanent marker to write a holiday greeting on the side of the flowerpot.*

* May need adult help or supervision.

Garden Marker

Use a wooden paint stick and a plastic lid to add color to the yard or garden.

Before Beginning Cover the printed side of the lid with contact paper. Cut two horizontal slits in the lid, approximately one-half inch apart.*

Make Your Great Gift

1. Decorate the paint stir stick with the craft foam pieces.
2. Using the craft foam, decorate the side of the lid covered with contact paper.
3. On the blank side of the lid, use the permanent marker to write a title or greeting such as "Grandma's Garden" or "Welcome."*
4. Slide the lid onto the stick through the horizontal slits in the lid. Position the lid so that it is at the top end of the stick and the printed greeting is visible.

Materials

plastic margarine lid
colored contact paper
scissors
wooden paint stir stick
self-adhesive craft foam, cut into small geometric shapes*
non-toxic permanent marker

Seasonal Suggestions

- Gardens are associated with springtime, making this a great Mother's Day gift. Tie a packet of inexpensive flower seeds to the garden marker, along with a copy of the following poem:*
  Roses are red and violets are blue.
  I think you are terrific.
  Happy Mother's Day to you!
- Self-adhesive foam can be purchased at most craft or fabric stores in a variety of bright, seasonal colors. Consider cutting the foam into holiday shapes, such as hearts or flowers.

---

* May need adult help or supervision.

Love Bug Plant Stake

Say, "I love you" with this indoor plant decoration made from a craft stick and Styrofoam.

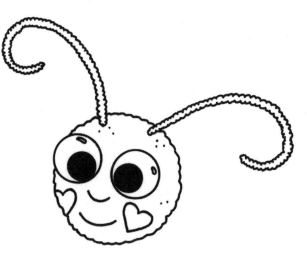

Materials

two wiggly eyes
pipe cleaners, cut into
   3" pieces*
small paper hearts
heart-shaped confetti
glue
Styrofoam ball, several
   inches in diameter
craft stick
ribbon

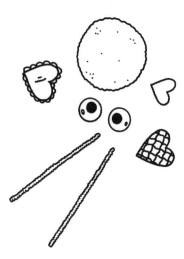

Make Your Great Gift

1. Create a "love bug" by gluing two wiggly eyes, a variety of pipe cleaners, and heart-shaped collage materials onto the Styrofoam ball.
2. After the bug is dry, push the ball onto the end of a craft stick and secure with a few drops of glue.*
3. When the plant stake is completely dry, attach a copy of the following poem to the craft stick using ribbon:*

   This little love bug is from me to you.
   She sits in your plants and carries a special message, too.
   Every time you see her, watching all you do,
   She is your reminder that I love you!

Helpful Hint

■ Make this gift extra special by placing it inside a small flowering plant.

* May need adult help or supervision.

Mini Birdbath

Plastic bottles come together to create a mini birdbath.

Before Beginning Cut off the neck portion of one of the 2-liter clear plastic bottles that has already been cut off five inches from the top (adult only).

Make Your Great Gift

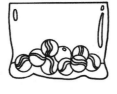

1. Decorate the outside of the cut portion with non-toxic oil pastels. Add lots of color.
2. Push the decorated piece into another cut top from a 2-liter plastic bottle (with neck remaining). This will protect the oil pastel decoration.
3. Screw a plastic lid to the decorated funnel shape. Set aside.
4. Place a variety of materials into the base of the cut-off bottom portion of the 1-liter bottle. This will serve as the birdbath stand. Fill it about half full, allowing room for the birdbath top.
5. Push the decorated top with lid side down into the base containing decorative materials. Some may have to be moved slightly so that the top sets securely.*
6. Use a hot glue gun (adult only!) to fasten the pieces together. The birdbath is ready to fill with water!*

Helpful Hints

- Use sandpaper to sand any rough edges of plastic.
- Use remaining plastic bottle parts to make funnels for sand or water play. Use the remaining bases for making Mosaic Bottle Organizers (see page 64).
- Instead of putting water inside, fill with dirt and plant flowers to create a unique flower pot.

Materials

2-liter clear plastic bottle, cut off approximately 5" from top*

1-liter clear plastic bottle, cut off approximately 3" from bottom*

scissors or utility knife (adult use only)

non-toxic oil pastels

plastic bottle lids

materials to put in base, such as shredded Mylar, plastic beads, sequins, decorative marbles, aquarium rock, pebbles, and shells

glue gun (adult use only) and glue sticks

Watering Can

Gardeners will love this watering can made from a liquid laundry soap bottle, colored wire, and markers.

Materials

liquid laundry
   detergent bottle
sharp scissors or utility
   knife (adult only)
non-toxic permanent
   markers
hole punch

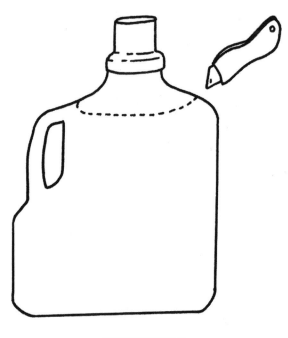

Before Beginning Cut off the top portion of the bottle, along the top ridge and just above the handle. Soak bottles in water to remove labels.*

Make Your Great Gift

1. Decorate the outside of the watering can with non-toxic permanent markers. Create a colorful picture or design.
2. Fill the watering can with homemade flowers (see pages 28-30), or fill the container with dirt and plant flowers or flower seeds inside.

Variation

■ Roll up pieces of tape and use them to attach flat plastic stencil shapes to the outside of the watering can. Apply non-toxic permanent marker in a zigzag motion around the edge of the stencils. Remove the stencils and add detail to the shape outlines.*

Helpful Hints

- Save cut-off tops for funnels to use in sand and water play.
- A utility knife works well for cutting off bottle tops, but be careful! (Utility knives are for adult use only.)
- Use Teflon scrapers or scrub brushes to remove residue from labels. This is fun to do outside in a tub of water.
- Use scraps of wallpaper, tissue paper, construction paper, and pipe cleaners to create a unique bouquet of flowers to place in the watering can.*

Seasonal Suggestion

- Fill the can with homemade flowers for a super Mother's Day, Grandparent's Day, Teacher Appreciation Day, or May Day gift.

Terra Cotta Music Makers

Charm a special person with beautiful chime music.

Materials

small clay pots, 1-3
  per child
paint
paintbrushes or sponge
  paintbrushes
clear acrylic spray paint
  (adult use only)
twine or rope, cut into
  1' to 2' lengths*
clapper, one per pot
  (old earrings, metal
  washers, or bell)

Make Your Great Gift

1. Paint the clay pot using a brush or sponge and various colors of tempera paint.
2. After the pot dries, spray it with clear acrylic paint to seal the tempera paint. (This must be done outside by adults only.)
3. Allow to dry. Repeat steps 1 and 2 to make additional pots.
4. Thread twine or rope through the hole in the clay pot.
5. Tie a knot right under the hole, allowing enough twine or rope to hang out of the bottom to attach the clapper.*
6. Thread the twine or rope through the clapper. Tie on the clapper, allowing it to hang freely inside the pot.*
7. Tie the pots together at the top end of the twine or rope, allowing them to hang freely.*

Helpful Hints

- When selecting pots, choose those that are smaller than a cup size, without any cracks or chips.
- Vary clapper types among pots to create diverse sounds.
- Paint a base coat using a sponge. When dry, paint detail with a paintbrush.*
- Add details by using dark-colored, non-toxic permanent markers on top of paint and acrylic coat.*

Seasonal Suggestion

- For Mother's Day, use pastel paint to create a beautiful and musical gift moms and grandmothers will enjoy. Use paint in warm, earth tones to make a Thanksgiving treasure for a loved one.

* May need adult help or supervision.

Wind Catcher

Add a splash of color to a porch with a wind catcher made from craft foam and yarn.

Materials

colored craft foam, approximately 9" x 17"

colored craft foam, cut into small shapes or pre-purchased shapes*

glue

ribbon, fabric strips or yarn, cut into 2' lengths*

hole punch

Make Your Great Gift

1. Glue small foam shapes onto one large piece of craft foam.
2. After the glue has dried, decide where to place the holes, and use a hole punch to put holes along one long edge of the craft foam. This will be the bottom of the wind catcher.*
3. String ribbon or yarn through the holes. Tie them into place, so they hang freely.*
4. Punch four holes along the top edge of the wind catcher at equal distances.*
5. Bring short edges of the large piece of foam together to form a tube shape. Glue or staple the edges together to secure the tube.*
6. Choose two pieces of yarn to string through the top four holes. Thread each piece of yarn through two holes opposite each other. Bring together the four loose ends to tie a knot. The wind catcher is ready to hang!*

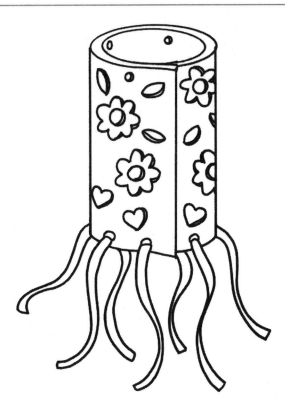

Helpful Hint

■ Other items that can be used to decorate the wind catcher include acrylic paint (older children), fabric scraps, felt pieces, or non-toxic permanent markers.*

Seasonal Suggestion

■ For winter holidays use glitter paint to decorate the top of a wind catcher and substitute foil gift ribbon for the wind catcher tails. Hang in a window to reflect the light.

* May need adult help or supervision.

Chapter 3

Come Play with Me

Share the gift of time with these great ideas that encourage family bonding.

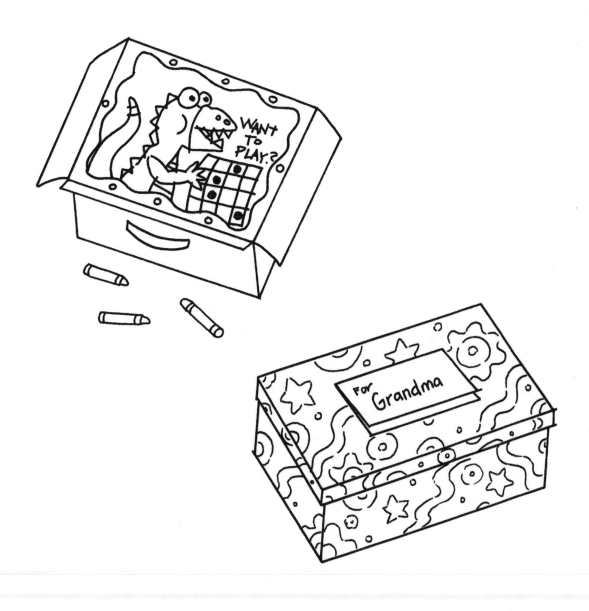

Picture Puzzles

Make a puzzle from a photograph for a very personal gift.

Materials

glue
photo of child
poster board or thin
    cardboard, cut into
    two 7" x 8"
    rectangles*
markers
paper lunch sack

Make Your Great Gift

1. Glue the photo to the middle of the piece of poster board or cardboard.
2. Using markers, decorate the poster board around the photo.
3. While the glue on the poster board dries, decorate a paper lunch sack with markers.
4. After the glue is dry, cut the poster board picture into six or eight pieces. Put the picture puzzle into the lunch sack. Include the second piece of blank poster board and a note encouraging the recipient to put the picture puzzle together with you, then use the other poster board to create a puzzle together.*

Helpful Hint

- Explain that the photo selected will be cut to make puzzle pieces. This may avoid an upset later on.

Seasonal Suggestions

- Before decorating the poster board square, write a brief message, such as "Happy Grandparent's Day," across the top.*
- Seasonal ink stamps and washable inkpads may be used to decorate the border of the picture puzzle.

* May need adult help or supervision.

I Spy Fun

Decorated tubes turn into hours of family fun.

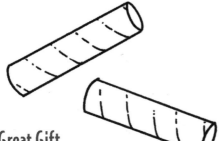

Make Your Great Gift

1. Decorate two sections of tube with paint.
2. After the paint dries, glue a variety of collage materials, including wiggly eyes, to the tubes.
3. When the tubes are completely dry, place both tubes in a plastic bag along with a copy of the following poem and game instructions:*

   I spy someone very special to me.
   A person who is lots of fun, too.
   Someone I like to play games with.
   And that special person is you!

How to Play "I Spy"

As you each look through the tubes, describe objects that you see. Talk about the color, shape, and size of the objects and try to guess what the other person sees.

Other ideas:

- Look for objects that are a certain color or shape. For example, see how many round objects you can find in two minutes.
- Look at each other and describe something that the other person is wearing.
- Look out the window and describe items that are found outdoors.

Helpful Hint

- Play "I Spy" with the child to give her a chance to learn how the game is played. This will help her to explain the game to the recipient of the gift and play it successfully with him or her.

Materials

cardboard wrapping paper tube, cut into 6" sections*
paint
paintbrushes
glue
collage materials
wiggly eyes
large zipper-seal plastic bag

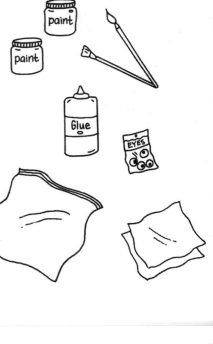

* May need adult help or supervision.

Play-with-Me Game Box

Turn a box into a traveling game container to share with anyone...anywhere.

Materials

box with flip top lid
    (shoebox, clean
    laundry detergent
    box)
sandpaper, as needed
black paint, in shallow
    pan
small roller paintbrush
non-toxic oil pastels
games

Make Your Great Gift

1. Use sandpaper on boxes that have a glossy finish or add a few drops of dish soap to the paint to help it adhere to the box.
2. Use a small roller paintbrush to paint the lid and sides of the box with black paint.
3. Allow the paint to dry completely.
4. Decorate the top and sides of the box with non-toxic oil pastels. Personalize the box by titling it, such as "Mueller Grab-It-and-Go Game Box."*
5. Fill the container with small, ready-made, or homemade games. Give as a gift for summer family travel, a trip to grandparents, or holiday break time.

Helpful Hint

■ Spray oil pastel drawings with a light coat of hairspray to prevent smearing (adult only). Use the hairspray away from children.

Game Ideas*

Tick-Tack-Toe

- Draw a tick-tack-toe grid on the inside of the box lid using markers.
- Create game pieces by using juice lids or poker chips, 10 per game.
- Stick garage sale circle dots onto the game pieces. Choose two colors and put five of each on a corresponding game piece.
- Use non-toxic permanent markers to add features to the dots. Make creatures, people, designs, or anything else the imagination dreams up.
- Store the pieces inside the game box sealed in a zipper-seal plastic sandwich bag.

Juice Box Memory

- Save, clean out, and cut fronts off of juice box containers.
- Find matching pairs of juice box fronts, enough to make six to nine pairs.
- To play, lay the juice box fronts face down, lift two at a time, and try to find a match.
- Store the pieces inside the game box sealed in a zipper-seal plastic sandwich bag.
  Option: Collect metal juice lids or other lids, and pairs of stickers. Put one sticker on each lid; use as above.

Pick-Up Sticks

- Make pick-up sticks using colorful drink stirrers or coffee stirrers.
- Play the game by dropping the sticks in a pile on the floor. Take turns pulling sticks out of the pile, one at a time, until one player's stick causes another stick to move. The goal is to remove sticks without causing the remaining sticks to move. Each player keeps the sticks they remove as points. Play until all the sticks are picked up.

* May need adult help or supervision.

Take-Along Art Box

Creative fun = a simple painted box and art materials.

Materials

box with lid, shoebox
   size or larger
zipper-seal plastic
   sandwich bags
art supplies, such as
   Styrofoam pieces,
   paper and wrapping
   paper scraps,
   stickers, craft foam
   scraps, yarn and
   ribbon scraps, toilet
   paper tubes, tissue
   paper scraps, felt
   scraps, contact
   paper scraps, and
   colored plastic lids
sandpaper, as needed
paint
paintbrushes
glitter glue

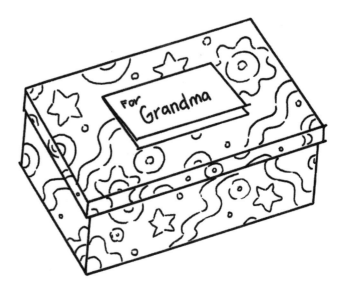

Make Your Great Gift

1. Lightly sand the lid and sides of the box if it has a glossy finish.
2. Paint the top and sides of the box.
3. Use glitter glue to add simple designs and highlights.
4. While the box is drying stuff art materials (see suggestions in the material list) into zipper-seal plastic bags.
5. After the box dries place the bagged materials inside the box and put on the lid. Attach a note such as:*
   There is a place for you in my heart
   Can we get together and just do art?
6. The box is ready to share with someone special.

Seasonal Suggestion

■ Decorate the box in glitter paint, add a festive bow, and fill with creative art supplies that you and a parent, grandparent, or caregiver could spend time with over the winter or summer break.

* May need adult help or supervision.

Coupon Pocket

Give someone the gift of time using homemade coupons.

Make Your Great Gift

1. Think about what kinds of activities the recipient enjoys, and what activities you and the recipient could do together. Include activities that are helpful to the recipient, as well as ideas that are recreational. Activity ideas could include:
   - cooking dinner
   - doing yard work
   - washing the car
   - going to the library
   - reading a book
   - going out for ice cream
   - making a picture for someone
   - going for a walk

2. These activities are to be done together, so be sure the wording of the coupon reflects that sentiment. For example, "This coupon is good for one evening of making dinner together."

3. Write five or six selected activities on the index cards.*

4. Use markers to decorate the blank side of each coupon.

5. Decorate the library pocket using the glue and sequins.

6. Place a piece of magnetic tape on the back of the pocket and place the coupons inside.

Materials

unlined index cards, 4" x 6", cut in half length-wise*
markers
library pocket
magnetic tape
glue
sequins

Seasonal Suggestion

- Consider selecting activities that are appropriate for the holiday or time of year. For example, in many places, a coupon for "help in the garden" would not be useful in December, but one for a "snow cone" making party would be very well received.

* May need adult help or supervision.

Family Activity Calendar

Help a family survive a holiday or summer break with this calendar full of fun and educational activity ideas.

Materials

copies of a blank
monthly calendar
construction paper, two
9" x 12" sheets
yarn
glue
markers or crayons
hole punch

 Before Beginning Make photocopies of a blank monthly calendar.*

Make Your Great Gift

1. Write or type a simple activity in each blank calendar square. Activities should be ones that the family members can do together easily without special materials. Activity ideas include:*

- make dinner together
- go to the library
- read a favorite book
- have a picnic
- make playdough
- make bubble soap and blow bubbles
- write a letter to a friend or relative
- look through family photos
- go on a nature walk
- draw a family portrait
- make sock puppets and put on a puppet show
- dance to music
- write your own fairy tale
- build an indoor obstacle course to crawl through
- make an indoor tent with a sheet and chairs
- trace each other's hands on paper
- make binoculars out of cardboard tubes
- play and build with empty boxes
- make fruit salad
- read a new book
- act out a favorite story or nursery rhyme
- paint with water outside
- make lemonade
- hunt for bugs outside
- play "Follow the Leader"
- make masks from paper plates

* May need adult help or supervision.

- make leaf rubbings play hide-and-seek
- listen to the sounds outside and write down what you hear

2. Glue the completed calendar to a blank piece of construction paper.*
3. Use the hole punch to make a hole near the top corners of the calendar page.*
4. Select one piece of construction paper, position it lengthwise, and draw a picture on it with crayons or markers.*
5. Punch two holes near the bottom corners of the construction paper picture, using the holes on the calendar page as a guide.*
6. Attach the picture to the calendar by laying both pages flat on a table, the picture directly above the calendar page. Loop a short piece of yarn through one hole on each page, then repeat on the other set of holes.*

Helpful Hints

- Select activities appropriate for the season and weather.
- Include pages with favorite recipes for playdough, bubble solution, and favorite snacks.*
- It is okay to repeat some activities within the same month. In fact, repeating activities, such as reading a favorite book or going to the library can be quite enjoyable.

* May need adult help or supervision.

Sing-a-Long Book and Tape

Make an audiotape of a child singing favorite songs.

Materials

blank audiotape with
    clear plastic case
tape recorder
white copy paper, some
    cut into 2¼" x 4"
    pieces*
photocopy machine
golf ball
paint
shoebox
permanent marker

Make Your Great Gift

1. Make an audio recording, singing your favorite songs.*
2. Place a 2¼" x 4" piece of white copy paper inside a small shoebox.
3. Add a golf ball and several drops of various colors of paint to the box.
4. Close the lid and shake the box for several seconds.
5. Remove the paper, and let the paint dry.
6. Use a permanent marker to write a title across the front of the painted paper; for example: "Alex, Live!"*
7. Place the paper inside the audiotape case to create the cover.*
8. Type the words to all the songs on the tape and make them into a booklet, including a note encouraging the recipient to spend time singing with you.*

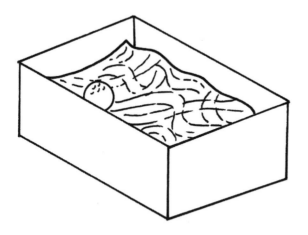

Helpful Hints

■ This activity makes a wonderful keepsake.
■ Practice your favorite songs and do your best when it is time to make the recording.*

Seasonal Suggestions

■ The tape and songbook can make a wonderful winter holiday gift. Sing winter songs and Christmas carols and include the words in the booklet. Use shiny, metallic colors of paint to create a festive cover for the audiotape.
■ Use patriotic songs for the Fourth of July and create a red, white, and blue cover.
■ The sing-along tape makes a treasured gift for grandparents (or other family members) who live far away and do not see their grandchildren regularly.

Family Story Notebook

Encourage time together with a homemade storybook.

Materials

three-hole punch
white copier paper
three-ring binder
markers or crayons
non-toxic black
    permanent marker

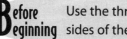 **Before Beginning**   Use the three-hole punch to make holes along the sides of the white paper.*

Make Your Great Gift

1. Think of a story and draw pictures to make a book using the white paper with the holes in the sides.
2. Dictate a statement or story about the pictures. Write these along the top or bottom of the pictures using the black permanent marker.*
3. Place the pages into the three-ring binder, along with 10 (or more) blank pages.
4. Decorate a white piece of paper without holes using the markers. Write "Family Story Notebook." Many binders have a clear cover pocket in which a cover page can be inserted. If this is not the case, use clear contact paper to adhere this cover page to the front of the notebook.*
5. Include a note in the front of the binder explaining that you wrote this story and that the blank paper is included so that others in the family can write a story together, or continue the one that you began. Consider placing a divider between your story and the blank pages.*

Seasonal Suggestion

■ Write a story about a holiday or event. Then decorate the
notebook cover page with seasonal stickers and markers in
holiday colors.

"Come Cook with Me" Jar

Create a lovely gift that contains a yummy recipe.

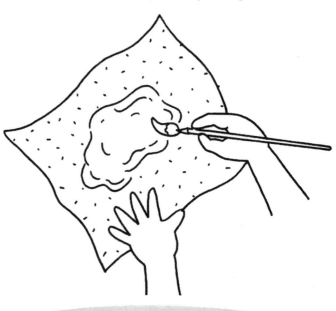

Materials

index card or paper,
   3" x 5"
recipe
muslin fabric, cut into
   7" squares*
washable markers
water
paintbrushes
quart jar with lid
glue
rubber bands
paper punch
ribbon

Before Beginning Type out or photocopy recipe (page 60) and glue to an 3" x 5" card or piece of paper. Demonstrate what happens when muslin is decorated with washable markers and brushed over with water.

Make Your Great Gift

1. Decorate a piece of muslin with washable markers. Then brush over it with water.
2. After muslin dries, center it on the jar lid and secure it with glue.*
3. Put dry recipe ingredients (see page 58) into the jar by layers.
4. Screw lid on tightly and place rubber band around loose muslin to form ruffle look.*
5. Tie the recipe around the jar neck with ribbon by punching a hole in the card or paper and lacing the ribbon through. Put a message on the recipe card similar to the following:*
   Sugar is sweet.
   Honey is too.
   I'm so happy
   When I cook with you.
6. Now it's ready to send off to a parent or grandparent!

Helpful Hints

■ Recipes that lend themselves to this activity include a variety of dry ingredients (such as nuts, flour, cocoa, dry milk, chocolate chips, oats), which are put into the jar and few "wet" ingredients, which are added by the recipient. Adjust recipe amounts to fit into the quart space.*

■ Quart canning jars work well for this activity.

Seasonal Suggestion

■ Use a recipe that corresponds to a particular holiday such as dry hot chocolate mix or bean soup mix for winter holidays. Top it off with muslin painted with glitter paint and a recipe card decorated with glitter crayon.

* May need adult help or supervision.

Oatmeal Bar Cookies

Use to fill "Come Cook with Me" Jars.

Materials

(for each quart jar)
quart glass jar
flour, ¾ cup*
baking soda,
    ¼ teaspoon*
salt, ¼ cup*
quick oats, 4 cups*
brown sugar, 1 cup*
chopped nuts or candy
    covered chocolate
    pieces, ¼ cup
    (be aware of any
    allergies)*
measuring spoons and
    cups
wide-mouth funnel
    (optional)
bowl
spoons

Make Your Great Gift

1. Wash hands with soap and water.
2. Measure and mix together flour, baking soda, and salt in a bowl. Pour half of this mixture into jar and pack down with spoon.*
3. Measure and pour in half of oats required. Pack down with spoon.*
4. Measure and pour in half of brown sugar. Pack down with spoon.*
5. Measure and pour in all of chopped nuts or chocolate pieces.*
6. Pour in remaining ingredients in order, flour mix, oats, and brown sugar. Reminder: pack down between each added ingredient.*
7. Put on the decorated lid.
8. Attach recipe on the following page.*

Helpful Hints

■ Use a wide-mouth canning funnel to help pour ingredients into the jar or make a substitute for the wide-mouth funnel by cutting off (adult only) the top portion of a 2-liter bottle. Then cut off the bottleneck just below the base to enlarge the hole. Invert it and use it as a funnel.*
■ Put the recipe (see below) on a 3″ x 5″ index card. Decorate by using markers and/or colored pencils.*

Seasonal Suggestion

■ This activity can be used for a variety of holidays and occasions by varying the recipes used. A hot chocolate mix or spice tea mix would be great for winter holidays. A layered trail mix is great for Father's Day or for summer traveling fun.

Do-Together Oatmeal Bar Cookies

Dry mix from quart jar
¾ cup butter or margarine
¼ cup white or dark corn syrup
1 teaspoon vanilla
Glass mixing bowls
Mixing spoon

1. Pour dry mix from jar into bowl and stir.
2. Put butter or margarine, syrup, and vanilla into another glass mixing bowl. Melt in a microwave by cooking for 15–20 seconds and stirring until liquid. This can also be done on the stovetop in a cooking pan.*
3. Remove from the microwave and add dry ingredients. Mix thoroughly.*
4. Press dough into the bottom of 9″ x 13″ pan.*
5. Bake at 350° for about 10 minutes or until lightly browned.*
6. Remove from oven and with metal spatula cut into desired shape. Let cool before removing from pan.*
7. Share with each other and a glass of milk! Yum!

* May need adult help or supervision.

Pack a Snack

Start the day off right with a healthy snack in a decorated bag.

Make Your Great Gift

1. Draw on both sides of the lunch sack using crayons or markers.
2. Write a short note in the bag asking for a "date" that evening to do an activity together, such as read a book or go for a walk.*
3. Put the snack into the lunch sack along with the note.
4. Give the sack to Mom, Dad, or anyone else at the beginning of a busy day.

Materials

paper lunch sack
crayons or markers
notepaper
pen
snack

Helpful Hints

- Prepare a simple snack food, such as trail mix.*
- If the snack includes food that is messy or might melt, place it in a plastic sandwich bag before placing it inside the paper sack.
- No time to make a healthy snack? Put a piece of fruit, such as an apple, banana, or orange, in the bag.

Seasonal Suggestions

- Use holiday ink stamps and washable inkpads to decorate the sack.
- Use a hole punch to make holes around the top edge of the paper sack. Lace ribbon in holiday colors through the holes in the bag.*
- Include a holiday napkin with the snack.

* May need adult help or supervision.

Chapter 4

Office Originals

Create gifts for a home or office space that are both fun and useful.

Weaving Band Pencil Holder

Not just for making potholders! Use weaving bands and plastic containers to create a colorful office organizer.

Materials

weaving bands
sturdy, plastic, open-mouth jar or cup
office supplies, such as pencils and small sticky note pads

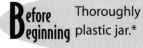

Before **B**eginning   Thoroughly clean the plastic jar.*

Make Your Great Gift

1. Stretch a variety of colored weaving bands around the outside of the jar or cup to create designs.
2. Place pencils or other office supplies in the jar.

Helpful Hint

■ To cut down on the cost of purchasing weaving bands at a craft store, use colored rubber bands instead. The rubber bands are harder to stretch and manipulate, so consider the age and fine motor ability of the child before using them.

Variation

■ Instead of a jar or cup, use plastic ketchup bottles. Stretch the bands around the wide base of the bottle. The narrow mouth of the bottle is perfect for flowers and creates a colorful vase. This vase can be used with the homemade flowers found on pages 28-30.

Seasonal Suggestions

■ Add a special message, such as "Happy Grandparent's Day," to a sticky note and secure it under a band on the outside of the jar.*
■ Holiday pencils and pens can be purchased at many educational and party supply stores to add a holiday touch to this gift.

* May need adult help or supervision.

Craft Foam Pencil Critter

Add personality to a plain pencil with craft foam.

Before **B**eginning   Cut two one-quarter inch long horizontal slits in the foam shapes approximately three-quarters of an inch apart.*

Materials

colored craft foam, cut into animal or person shapes
glue
yarn, cut into 1 ½" pieces*
wiggly eyes, and small buttons
small thin tip markers
pencils, unsharpened
paper, cut into 1" x 4" strips*

Make Your Great Gift

1. Add features to the craft foam shape using glue, yarn, wiggly eyes, buttons, and markers.
2. Slip a pencil through the two slits in the craft foam topper.
3. Write personal messages on thin slips of paper and tape them to the pencil.*

Helpful Hints

- Use fabric tube paint or tempera paint in squeeze bottles to add features.
- Use cookie cutters or a die-cut machine to cut out the shapes.

Seasonal Suggestions

- Vary the shapes to fit any occasion. For example, use turkey shapes for Thanksgiving. Use washable stamp pads to add fingerprint "feathers" to the turkey.
- "Person" shapes could become a grandma or grandpa for Grandparent's day.

* May need adult help or supervision.

Mosaic Bottle Organizers

Make an organizer with tissue paper, liquid starch, and plastic bottles.

Materials

1-liter or 2-liter plastic bottles, cut at half-bottle length*
dark colored tissue paper, cut in approximately 1" squares or triangles*
liquid starch
thick paintbrushes

 Before Beginning Demonstrate how to create a mosaic effect on the plastic bottles by applying a coat of liquid starch and placing the tissue paper squares slightly apart from each other to create a pattern.*

Make Your Great Gift

1. Create a mosaic design on the bottle, filling the space on the sides of the bottle.
2. After the squares are slightly dry, apply a light topcoat of liquid starch, being careful not to move the design.*
3. Allow the bottle to dry.
4. Fill the bottle with a gift or make several to use as office organizers.

Helpful Hints

- Sand rough edges of cut bottles with sandpaper.*
- Glue several bottles to a cardboard or matte board base to use as an organizer.

Seasonal Suggestions

- Use green/red tissue paper for Christmas or blue/white tissue paper for Hanukkah to create a grouping of organizers mounted on matte board. They could be used to hold cards, stamps, pens, and other supplies for the holidays.
- Get ready for visiting grandparents by creating a set filled with things to do together. For example: crayons, scissors, a package of playdough, collage materials, and other art materials.

* May need adult help or supervision.

Made-It-Myself Mouse Pad

Impress a computer user with a unique mouse pad.

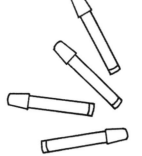

Materials

white or light colored craft foam, cut into approximately 8" x 9" pieces*

non-toxic permanent colored markers

clear vinyl, cut the same size and shape as craft foam

clear 2" wide book or packing tape, cut to 9" length*

Make Your Great Gift

1. Brainstorm ideas to draw on the mouse pad. Possible ideas include:
   - drawing a scene for the "mouse" to travel through
   - traced simple shapes
   - a self-portrait
2. Draw the design on one side of the craft foam with the permanent markers.
3. Place a piece of tape approximately 9" long to adhere clear vinyl to craft foam along the top long edge. Then you can slide notes, memos, or photos between the vinyl and the foam.*
4. Trim as needed.*

Helpful Hints

- Add notes and photos under the clear vinyl.
- Clear vinyl, sold by the yard, may be found at stores that sell fabric.
- Use stencils to trace and cut out a mouse pad.

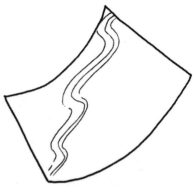

Seasonal Suggestion

- Make a personal mouse pad by putting the name of the recipient on the craft foam. This makes a great end-of-year gift for teachers.*

* May need adult help or supervision.

Sticky Note Magnet

Make a useful note pad magnet with a special surprise message.

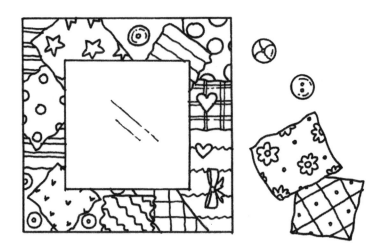

Materials

poster board, cut into a
  5" x 5" square*
sticky notes, 3" x 3"
lightweight collage
  materials
glue
magnetic tape
narrow-tip marker

Make Your Great Gift

1. Place a sticky note in the middle of the poster board square.
2. Glue lightweight collage materials around the edges of the poster board, avoiding the area covered by the sticky note. Suggested collage materials include tissue paper and wrapping paper scraps, confetti, small buttons, feathers, craft foam shapes, ribbon, and fabric scraps.
3. After the glue dries, write a short message, such as "I love you, Mom!" to the person receiving the gift. Take the sticky note off of the collage and write this message in the blank space in the middle of the poster board.*
4. Take a short stack of sticky notes and stick them on top of the dictated message. This special message will be revealed when the last sticky note is taken off for use.
5. Add a small strip of magnetic tape to the back of each corner of the poster board. The note pad can now be placed on a refrigerator or file cabinet.

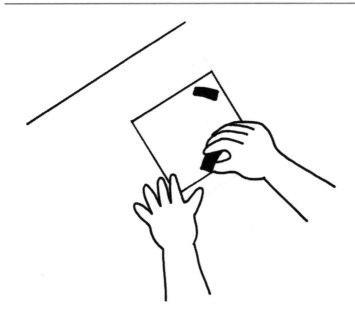

Helpful Hints

■ To create a sturdier magnet, use thick cardboard from an old box instead of poster board.

■ Use a shallow dish of glue and a cotton swab to spread the glue. This will prevent saturating the small piece of poster board with too much glue.

Seasonal Suggestion

■ Write a seasonal message to be revealed when the last sticky note is used. For example, for a Thanksgiving gift write "I am thankful for you!"*

Clip-to-It Board

Create a useful writing surface with a piece of cardboard, paint, and clip.

Materials

thick cardboard, cut
    into 9" x 12" pieces*
paint, thinned slightly
    with water
paintbrushes
metal bulldog clip
non-toxic permanent
    markers

Make Your Great Gift

1. Paint the cardboard lightly. (Don't apply too much paint because the surface should be as smooth as possible.)
2. After the surface is dry, write messages to the recipient on top of the painted area using non-toxic permanent markers. Examples include: "Mommy's Message Board," "Daddy's Doodles," "Mr. (Mrs.) _____ Memos," or another appropriate message.*
3. Attach the bulldog clip to the top of the finished clipboard.
4. Attach a few sheets of paper with the clip to create a useful gift for anyone.

Helpful Hints

- Masonite, available from home improvement stores, is a sturdy substitute for cardboard. Blank clipboards may also be an option.
- Use paint pens to draw pictures as an alternative to using paint.
- Sponges or handprints can be used to apply the paint instead of a brush.
- Make half-sized boards to use for holding shopping or "to do" lists.

Seasonal Suggestion

- This clipboard makes a useful gift for anyone who works in an office, keeps lists at home, or needs a communication board. Personalize it with a name to make a handy Father's Day gift, teacher's gift, or Grandparent's Day gift.

Creative Calendar

A clear report cover and a few stickers turn a simple calendar into a desk decoration.

Materials

clear plastic report
   cover
seasonal stickers
computer-generated
   calendar on 8½" x
   11" paper*

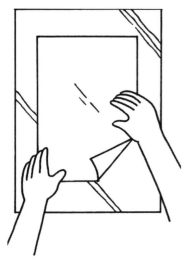

Make Your Great Gift

1. Place a piece of paper on top of the report cover, leaving only a one-inch border of the cover exposed.*
2. Decorate the exposed edges of the report cover with a variety of stickers.
3. Remove the paper from the top of the cover and insert the paper calendar into the report cover. Position the calendar so that is visible through the transparent cover and is framed by the stickers.

Variation

- Use glue and flat collage materials instead of stickers.

* May need adult help or supervision.

Corky Note Board

Make a bulletin board out of cork, cardboard, and paint.

Materials

paint

shallow dishes

thin sheets of cork, cut in 5" x 7" pieces or larger*

two pieces of thick cardboard, cut to size of cork

sponge shapes

collage materials, such as buttons, colored foam shapes, and stickers

yarn, cut to 8" or larger piece

glue

Make Your Great Gift

1. Put a small amount of paint in each shallow dish.
2. Decorate the sheet of cork by making sponge prints on one side.
3. After the paint dries, glue collage materials on the cork to form a border around the edge. Allow glue to dry.
4. Glue two pieces of equal-sized cardboard on top of each other to double the thickness.
5. Construct a hanger by poking two holes close to one edge of the cardboard pieces and stringing with yarn.*
6. Glue the decorated cork sheet on top of cardboard pieces. Allow to dry.*

Helpful Hint

■ Rolls or sheets of cork can be found at fabric, home improvement, craft, and hobby stores.

Seasonal Suggestions

■ Cut corkboard into shapes that are appropriate for various gift-giving occasions. For example, a tree shape at Christmas, or a car or tie shape for Father's Day.*

■ Small, decorated pieces of corkboard without cardboard backing make lovely ornaments and wall hangings! Add some jewels or sequins for a unique gift.

* May need adult help or supervision.

Layer Jar Paperweight

Produce an elaborate paperweight and boredom buster.

Materials

honey
light or dark corn syrup
cooking oil
water (can be colored
    with food coloring)
large baby food jars
    with lids, clean
    and dry*
funnel
measuring spoons
assorted items that sink
    and float
masking tape
brown shoe polish
sponge brush
scissors
glue gun (adult only)
    and glue sticks

Make Your Great Gift

1. Pour the four liquids into a baby food jar, one at a time. Use measuring spoons to put equal portions of two tablespoons of each liquid. Use a funnel to help pour liquids into the jar. Wipe spills off the side of the jar.*
2. Drop assorted items that sink and float into jar.
3. Cut pieces of masking tape and place them over the jar lid.
4. Coat the tape with the shoe polish, using a sponge brush if necessary. Allow the polish to dry.
5. Secure the lid by adhering with a glue gun (adult only).

Helpful Hint

■ If concerned about using glass jars, substitute clear eight-ounce water bottles.

* May need adult help or supervision.

Jiffy Juice Lid Magnet

Create a durable magnet with metal juice lids, nuts, and bolts.

Materials

metal juice can lids, such as from frozen orange juice

magnetic tape, cut into pieces

nuts, washers, and screws (assorted small sizes)

glue

Make Your Great Gift

1. Create a design by positioning the nuts, screws, and washers on a metal juice lid. Think how they can be used to create pictures (nuts for eyes, screws for mouth, and so on).
2. Glue the pieces on the juice lid.
3. When glue is dry, secure a piece of magnetic tape to the back.*

Variations

■ For added color, spray paint lids and/or some of the nuts, screws, and washers before or after they are glued together. Caution: An adult should always do spray painting, far away from children.

■ Other things that could be glued to the lids include colored craft foam or colored poster board petals, with a photo positioned in the middle.

Seasonal Suggestion

■ For a winter holiday gift, use three metal juice lids and nuts, screws, and washers or other materials to create a snowman. One lid becomes the head and the other two become the body of the snowman. Secure magnetic tape to each lid. Spray paint white (adult only). Stick on any metal surface to "make" a snowman.*

* May need adult help or supervision.

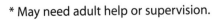

Matte Board Magnet

Use framing scraps to create lively magnets.

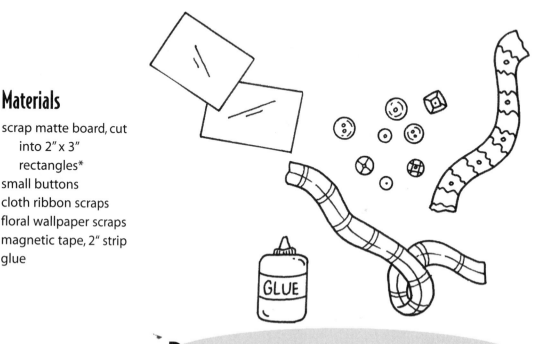

Materials

scrap matte board, cut
    into 2" x 3"
    rectangles*
small buttons
cloth ribbon scraps
floral wallpaper scraps
magnetic tape, 2" strip
glue

Before Beginning Collect scrap matte board from the local frame shop or craft store. Cut the scrap into 2" x 3" rectangles.*

Make Your Great Gift

1. Glue the buttons, ribbon, and wallpaper on the matte board.
2. Place a strip of magnetic tape across the back of the matte board.

Variation

■ Add a bar pin to the back of the matte board in place of the magnet tape to create a unique piece of jewelry.*

Helpful Hints

■ If matte board is not readily available, use thick cardboard instead.
■ Select small collage materials that are lightweight.

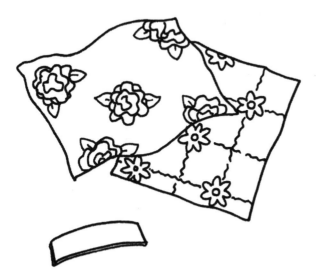

Variations

- Use paint instead of collage materials.
- The buttons and ribbon give this gift a country charm, but changing the collage materials can give the magnet a whole new look.

Seasonal Suggestions

- Glue small metal nuts to the board and attach a note that reads, "I Am Nuts About You!" for an anytime gift!*
- Use paint or a permanent marker to write a holiday greeting on the front of the magnet, such as "Happy July 4th!"*

---

* May need adult help or supervision.

Recycled Magnet

Reuse and recycle promotional magnets.

Materials

discarded promotional
magnets
colored fine-tipped
markers
cardstock or
construction paper,
cut slightly larger
than the magnet*
glue

Make Your Great Gift

1. Peel the paper surface off the magnet.*
2. Draw pictures and messages on the construction paper (for example, "Dad's Stuff" or "Mom's Notes").*
3. Glue the picture onto the magnet.*

Helpful Hints

■ Other mediums to use on the paper cover include washable stamp pads with fingerprints and markers to create creatures, or watercolor paints and markers.
■ Pictures can be laminated before gluing on the magnet for added durability.*
■ Put magnet inside a homemade card to give as a gift.

* May need adult help or supervision.

Family Foam Magnets

Create these magnets made from craft foam, wiggly eyes, and ribbon scraps.

Materials

craft foam, various colors, cut into a variety of people shapes*

craft foam shapes

wiggly eyes or small buttons

non-toxic permanent markers

scissors

glue

yarn, cut into small pieces

ribbon, lace, or fabric scraps

magnetic tape, cut into pieces*

Make Your Great Gift

1. Choose several craft foam people.
2. Add facial features using wiggly eyes or small buttons and non-toxic permanent markers.
3. Cut craft foam pieces into triangles, rectangles, and squares to create clothes with these shapes. Glue to craft foam people.*
4. Use yarn pieces and other scraps to create hair or decoration for clothing.
5. Allow foam people to dry. Attach magnetic tape to the back of each figure. Magnets hold memos, photos, or artwork!

Helpful Hints

- Glitter glue or wallpaper scraps can be used instead of foam scraps to create "clothing."
- Offer simple, cookie-cutter people shapes or stencil shapes to trace and cut.

Seasonal Suggestions

- Use brown craft foam and small buttons to create gingerbread family magnets for a winter holiday.
- Attach bar pins to back of the foam people and give away for Mother's Day.

* May need adult help or supervision.

Stress Ball Sock

Turn a tube sock into a tension-breaking gift.

Materials

non-toxic permanent
   markers in a variety
   of colors
new, white, adult-size,
   knee-length athletic
   sock
sand
two zipper-seal plastic
   sandwich bags
plastic tray
masking tape

Before Beginning Stretch the sock tight and tape it to the plastic tray.*

Make Your Great Gift

1. Draw on the socks with a variety of non-toxic permanent markers. (Protect clothing!)
2. Scoop sand into a plastic sandwich bag. Place the bag of sand inside another sandwich bag and tape closed.
3. Place the sealed bag of sand inside the toe of the sock.
4. Tie a knot in the ankle of the sock to secure the bags of sand in place.*
5. Squeeze the newly created stress ball and enjoy how the sand feels.

Helpful Hints

- If sand is not available, other materials, such as gravel, flour, and salt can be used instead.
- Send this gift with directions for what to do if the sock begins to leak its contents. Instruct the recipient to simply untie the sock and place the broken bag of sand inside a new sandwich bag.*

Seasonal Suggestion

- The Stress Ball Sock makes a great gift for Father's Day.

* May need adult help or supervision.

Chapter 5

Household Helps

Give practical gifts that add enjoyment to everyday activities.

Personalized Coasters

Create personalized coasters out of vinyl shelf liner and permanent markers.

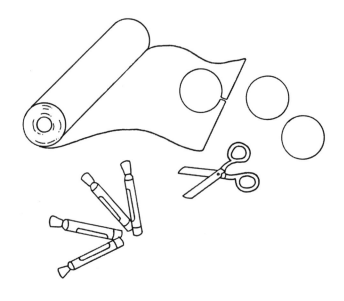

Materials

light, solid-colored vinyl
   shelf liner, cut into
   3" to 4" diameter
   circles*
non-toxic permanent
   markers

Make Your Great Gift

1. Make enough vinyl circles to make a coaster for each family member or gift recipient.
2. Use the non-toxic permanent markers to decorate the circles. Add facial features to each circle, or try to make each look like the recipient of the gift.
3. "Name" each coaster. Write the name on each coaster.*

Helpful Hints

■ Try permanent inkpads and small sponge shapes as a variation.

Seasonal Suggestion

■ To create a gift that is certain to cause conversations at a Thanksgiving dinner table, place the coasters inside a homemade card.

* May need adult help or supervision.

Beautiful Basket Liner

Add a touch of color to a bandana, line a basket, or use it to wrap up some goodies and create a festive gift.

Before Beginning Put paint in plastic bag(s) and seal shut. Use a different color of paint in each bag, as desired.*

Make Your Great Gift

1. Place a bandana flat inside a clean pizza box.
2. Secure fabric corners to the box with tape.
3. Place items to roll into the paint-filled bags, seal the bags, and shake to coat with paint. (Wear a paint smock.)*
4. Put the paint-coated items from the bags into the pizza box containing the bandana.
5. Seal the box shut with pieces of tape and shake the box.*
6. Remove tape, and carefully remove the bandana from the box. Dry flat overnight.*
7. Fold the bandana and tie a ribbon around it to present as a gift.*

Helpful Hints

- Substitute solid-colored fabric cut into 22" x 22" squares for the bandana. Fabric suggestions: cotton, non-stretch cotton /polyester, and muslin.
- Place bread, cookies, snack mix, or other items into a bandana-lined basket.
- Use a painted scarf to wrap another gift by pulling the scarf's edges around the gift and tying the scarf with ribbon.*

Seasonal Suggestion

- Vary colors of fabric and paint to fit any gift-giving occasion. For example, pastel colors can be used for May Day or Easter, and blue and silver or red and green for winter holidays.

Materials

solid-colored bandana
large, clean pizza box
fabric paint
things that roll (golf balls, Koosh balls, or marbles)
tape
zipper-seal plastic sandwich bags
ribbon, cut into 18" to 24" lengths*
paint smocks

---

* May need adult help or supervision.

Chip Clip

Decorate a clothespin and create a fun clip for sealing favorite munchies.

Materials

cardboard cut into a
   2" x 3" rectangle*
small stickers
markers
clothespin
glue
non-toxic permanent
   marker

Make Your Great Gift

1. Decorate the cardboard rectangle with stickers and markers.
2. Glue the decorated rectangle to one side of a clothespin.
3. After the glue dries, use the permanent marker to personalize the Chip Clip with the recipient's name. For example, "Dad's Chip Clip" can be written directly on the side of the clothespin or in a blank space on the decorated cardboard.*

Helpful Hint

■ Use other materials to decorate the cardboard. For example, use paint and collage materials to create a unique Chip Clip. Select flat materials such as paper and fabric scraps; materials that protrude from the clip will soon fall off with use.

Seasonal Suggestions

■ Cut the cardboard into simple shapes to make it more appropriate for a specific occasion. For a fun Father's Day gift, cut the cardboard into the shape of a necktie and glue fabric scraps from old neckties to the shape.*

■ The Chip Clip also makes a great gift for a patriotic holiday, when picnics and potato chips are especially popular. Provide red, white, and blue materials to decorate the clothespin and create the perfect July 4th present.

■ The clip can be placed on a small bag of homemade snacks, such as trail mix or cookies, which becomes part of the gift.

* May need adult help or supervision.

Candy Dish

Make a holiday candy dish using plastic flowerpot saucers.

Materials

two 6" clear plastic
flowerpot saucers
colored glue
tissue paper scraps,
ribbon, colored
paper scraps, and foil
scraps
photo of child
sandwich bag
seasonal candy

Make Your Great Gift

1. Drizzle colored glue around the inside of one of the saucers.
2. Place ribbon, tissue paper, colored paper, and foil scraps on the glue in the saucer.
3. Place several drops of glue in the middle of the saucer and place the photo on the glue.
4. Put the second saucer inside of the decorated saucer, pressing down firmly. The second saucer creates a protective layer over the photo and decorations, while leaving these items visible in the bottom of the dish. Let the glue in the candy dish dry for at least an hour.*
5. Place a handful of candies in a sandwich bag and tie with a ribbon. Put the bag of candy into the candy dish.

Helpful Hint

- Use only flat collage materials so that the two saucers fit together snuggly.

Variation

- Turn this candy dish into a colorful sun catcher! Use only colored tissue paper scraps to decorate the first saucer. Place the second saucer over the first and them let them dry for at least an hour. Turn the dish up on its side and make a hole in the top edge of the saucers. String yarn through the hole in the dish and hang in a window.

Seasonal Suggestions

■ Make a Christmas candy dish using collage materials such as shredded Mylar, foil confetti, ribbon, and wrapping paper scraps. Select red and green peppermint candies to place in the dish.

■ A springtime or Easter dish can be made using pastel collage materials and Easter grass. Place a bag of jellybeans in the dish.

Octopus Duster

Make cleaning fun with a duster made from a decorated tube sock.

Materials

men's white tube socks
pillow stuffing
rubber band
flat jewels and buttons
glue
dowel stick,
 approximately
 2' long*

 Before Beginning Cut into ribbed area of sock to form approximately eight strips, stopping half way through the length of sock. Cut a small hole in toe, big enough for the dowel to fit through.*

Make Your Great Gift

1. Stuff the toe area of the sock with pillow stuffing.
2. Secure the center of the sock just below the stuffed area with a rubber band.*
3. Glue jewels and buttons on for facial features and decoration. Dry.*
4. Put glue on the top part of the dowel stick and push it into the hole on the toe end of stuffed sock. Glue hole edges to the dowel. Dry.*
5. The Octopus Duster is ready to dust away cobwebs and high shelves. Include a note or poem such as the following:*

   Here is an octopus just for you
   To help with dusting that you do.
   If reaching high is the case
   Use his legs with a happy face.

Helpful Hint

■ Substitute plastic grocery bags for pillow stuffing.

Variation

■ Use ink daubers to create a polka-dotted creature.

* May need adult help or supervision.

Collage Bookmark

Create a simple, inexpensive bookmark appropriate for any special occasion.

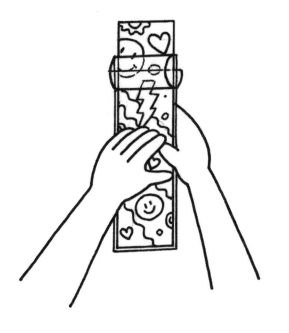

Materials

construction paper, cut into 1½" x 7" pieces*
glue stick
flat collage materials such as confetti, paper scraps, wallpaper scraps, and stickers
clear contact paper

Make Your Great Gift

1. Select a strip of construction paper.
2. Glue the flat collage materials to the construction paper strip.
3. After the glue dries, write a short message to the recipient on the back of the bookmark, including the date and your name.*
4. Cover the bookmark using clear contact paper.

Seasonal Suggestion

■ A Collage Bookmark makes a great gift for special people who live far away because it is small and lightweight, making it easy to mail. For Grandparent's Day, mail the homemade bookmark in a stamped, legal-size envelope.*

---

* May need adult help or supervision.

Craft Stick Bookmark

Craft sticks and craft foam make a colorful, personalized gift.

Materials

craft foam
large cookie cutter
scissors
craft foam scraps,
    variety of colors
glue
large craft stick
non-toxic permanent
    marker
pen or pencil

Before Beginning Cut a fun shape out of craft foam. Trace around a large cookie cutter and use scissors to cut out a simple shape such as a heart or star. The shape should be about three or four inches in diameter.*

Make Your Great Gift

1. Decorate the larger foam shape with glue and a colorful variety of smaller craft foam scraps.
2. While the glue dries, write a short message on a craft stick to the recipient of the bookmark. For example: "I love you, Mom!" or "You're the Best!" will easily fit in the given space. Use a permanent marker.*
3. Glue the foam shape to the end of the craft stick. Be sure not to cover up the greeting written on the stick.
4. On the back of the bookmark, write your name and the date using a permanent marker.*

Helpful Hint

- Be sure to select a short message that will fit on the craft stick. Consider writing a generic holiday greeting, such as "Happy Valentine's Day," on the bookmark.*

Seasonal Suggestions

- Packages of small craft foam pieces can be purchased at most craft stores, and come in a variety of seasonal characters and shapes.
- Select shapes for specific holidays, such as a flower for a spring holiday, a candle for a winter holiday, a leaf for a fall holiday, or a tie shape for Father's Day.

* May need adult help or supervision.

"Look What I Made!" Magnet

Display children's masterpieces using a clothespin.

Look what I made!

Before **B**eginning Print "Look What I Made!" across the top edge of the index card using a permanent marker.*

Materials

unlined index card,
   4" x 6"
permanent marker
flat collage materials
glue
clear contact paper
self-adhesive Velcro,
   2" strip
clothespin
magnetic tape, 2" strip
construction paper
crayons

Make Your Great Gift

1. Glue flat, lightweight collage materials, such as wallpaper scraps and foil confetti, to the index card.
2. Cover the index card with clear contact paper.*
3. Attach self-adhesive Velcro to the back of the index card and the front of the clothespin, fastening the card and pin together.*
4. Place a piece of magnetic tape on the back of the clothespin.
5. Draw a picture for the recipient of the gift using the construction paper and crayons and place it in the clip to be displayed.

Seasonal Suggestion

■ The "Look What I Made!" clip is a perfect Mother's Day present. Personalize Mom's gift by writing your name in place of the "I" in the title. Or change the title to "I Made This Just for Mom."*

* May need adult help or supervision.

Write-and-Wipe Board

Turn a magnetic photo album page into a dry-erase board.

Materials

white or light color
magnetic photo
album page
piece of paper, 1″
smaller than
album page
small foil wrapping
paper shapes, small
tissue paper shapes,
small stickers
yarn
dry-erase marker
magnetic tape, 2″ strip

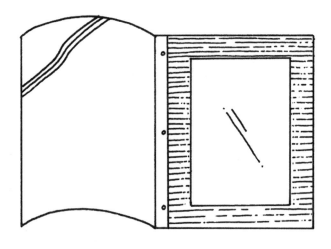

Make Your Great Gift

1. Peel the clear cover from the magnetic photo album page. Place a piece of paper in the middle of the page, leaving a one-inch margin around the edges of the album page.*
2. Place wrapping and tissue paper shapes and small stickers on the sticky surface of the album page around the paper.
3. Remove the paper from the center of the page and replace the clear page cover, pressing firmly to secure the collage materials. This should leave a large blank space in the middle of the page, with a decorative border around the edges.
4. Turn the album page lengthwise and string yarn through the binder holes on this side of the page. This will give the recipient a way to hang the wipe board.*
5. Write a short message or greeting on the wipe board using the dry-erase marker.*
6. Cut magnetic tape strip in half. Place one piece on the board and the other on the dry-erase marker. Attach the marker to the top of the board using the magnetic tape.*

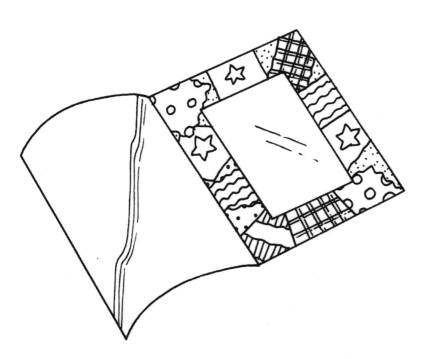

Helpful Hints

- The clear cover will not stick to the album page if collage materials are placed too close to the edges of the page. If this happens, simply secure the sides of the cover using clear tape.
- Add one or more small photos to the collage materials along the border of the wipe board.
- Magnetic tape may be added to the back of the album page to create a magnetic wipe board for the refrigerator.

French Memo Board

Turn a piece of cardboard into a holiday cardholder.

Materials

sturdy cardboard, cut
    into large 24"x 24"
    heart shape*
paint, several colors
foam sponge shapes
roll of ribbon, at least
    ½" wide
clear tape
masking tape

Before **B**eginning Cut notches around the edges of the cardboard heart. Place paint in several shallow containers.*

Make Your Great Gift

1. Decorate the cardboard heart using the foam sponge shapes and several different colors of paint.
2. After the paint dries, wind the ribbon randomly around the front and back of the heart. Each time the ribbon reaches the edge of the heart, slide it into one of the notches to secure it in place.*
3. Use clear tape to secure the ribbon on the back of the cardboard.
4. Write a special message to the recipient of the memo board on a card, and tuck it inside the ribbon on the board.*
5. Tape a loop of ribbon to the back of the board using masking tape. This gives the recipient a way to hang the memo board.*

Helpful Hints

■ It is important to use thick, sturdy cardboard for this project. Thin materials, such as poster board, will curl up, especially when the paint and ribbon are added.

■ If the cardboard has writing on it, use dark paint and a paintbrush to cover the cardboard completely before adding the sponge shape prints.

Seasonal Suggestions

■ Use this gift idea for holidays when greeting cards are usually exchanged.

■ Select seasonal sponge shapes and paint colors. For example, use flower shapes for a Mother's Day board, heart shapes for a Valentine's Day board, or stars and metallic paint for a winter holiday board.

Button-Up Bulletin Board

Trim an old shirt to create a unique and useful memo board.

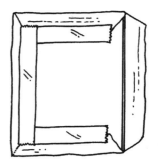

Materials

man's button-up shirt,
    in a light color
thick cardboard, cut
    into 12" x 18"
    rectangle*
masking tape
scissors
paint
sponge shapes
plastic or wooden
    buttons
glue
ribbon or yarn
pencil
small pad of paper

Before Beginning Thoroughly wash and dry the man's shirt. Place the cardboard rectangle inside the shirt, with the buttons and front shirt pocket laid evenly across the front of the cardboard. Cut out this section of the shirt, leaving two inches of extra fabric around the edges. Place the shirt piece evenly on the cardboard, and then tape the edges to the back of the cardboard using sturdy tape.*

Make Your Great Gift

1. Place the paint in shallow containers.
2. Decorate the front of the shirt board using paint and sponge shapes.
3. Use buttons and glue to add more decorations.
4. When the shirt is dry, turn the board over and use masking tape to attach a loop of ribbon or yarn to the back for easy hanging.*
5. Put a pencil and a small pad of paper in the shirt pocket on the front of the memo board.
6. Consider adding a title, such as "Grandma's Memo Board" or "Nick's Mom's Notes," near the top of the board using either paint or a permanent marker.*

Seasonal Suggestion

■ Write a special note to the recipient of the memo board. Write the note on colorful seasonal paper, then roll it up, and place it in the pocket on the memo board.*

* May need adult help or supervision.

Treasure Box

Recycled shirt boxes are the perfect place to store treasures.

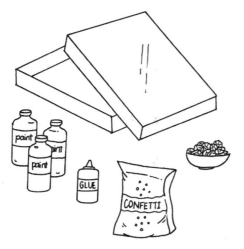

Materials

cardboard shirt box, with lid
paint
paintbrushes
plastic gemstones, sequins, or foil
confetti
glue

Make Your Great Gift

1. Paint the lid of the box and add the gemstones and sequins with glue, leaving space at one end of the lid to write the recipient's name.
2. After the lid is dry, place it on the shirt box.
3. Personalize the treasure box by writing the name of the recipient in the blank space on the lid. Personalize the box according to the holiday; for example, write "Mommy's Treasures" if it is a Mother's Day gift.*
4. This treasure box is the perfect size for storing artwork.

Helpful Hint

■ Stock up on inexpensive shirt boxes by purchasing them shortly after Christmas.

Seasonal Suggestions

■ Make a Valentine's Day treasure box by using heart-shaped sponges with red and pink paint. Then tuck a special valentine for a family member inside.
■ Make a unique treasure box for any holiday by making handprints on the box lids, and then adding collage materials.*

* May need adult help or supervision.

All Smiles Key Chain

Warm a heart with a precious key chain made from poster board, ink daubers, and a photo.

Materials

poster board or tag-
   board, cut into 4"
   diameter circles*
washable color ink
   daubers
colored pencils
hole punch
wallet-sized photo
   of child
glue stick
clear contact paper or
   laminating machine
small metal loop rings,
   used for key rings

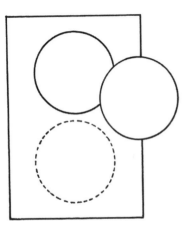

Make Your Great Gift

1. Use ink daubers to put dots on one side of the poster board circle.
2. When dry, use colored pencils to create characters out of ink circles. They could be turned into happy smiling faces, bugs, family members, clowns, and so on. Be creative!
3. Add a message.*
4. Glue the photo onto the opposite side.
5. Trim the photo as needed.*
6. Cover with contact paper or laminate.*
7. Use the hole punch to put a hole into the circle. Add a metal loop ring for keys to make this cheerful key ring for someone special.

Helpful Hints

■ Metal loop rings can be found at office supply stores.
■ Experiment with using other materials, such as paint, to
   decorate the key ring. Glue on sequins around the photo to
   add a border.

Seasonal Suggestion

■ Cut the poster board into a tree shape, heart, flower, or other
   shape. Decorate and cover as above, then slide through a
   piece of small beaded chain and close with a connector.
   Give as a ceiling fan pull or a holiday decoration.*

---

* May need adult help or supervision.

Car Visor Clip

Help someone special keep his or her car organized.

Materials

clothespin, spring type
library pocket
paint
cotton swabs or thin
   paintbrushes
glue
non-toxic permanent
   marker

Make Your Great Gift

1. Paint the clothespin and library pocket using both the cotton swabs or thin paintbrushes.
2. After the paint dries, glue the library pocket to one side of the clothespin.
3. Use the permanent marker to personalize the clip by writing a title on the library pocket such as "Dad's Car Clip."*
4. Include a note with the gift suggesting that the recipient clip it to the car visor and use the pocket for parking stubs or loose change.*

Helpful Hint

■ The library pocket will last longer if it is laminated or covered with clear contact paper before attaching it to the clothespin. Laminate does not adhere to other materials well, so use self-adhesive Velcro to attach the pocket to the clothespin.*

Variation

■ Add magnetic tape to the back of the clothespin to create a refrigerator clip that can hold papers. Use the library pocket for storing pens and pencils.

* May need adult help or supervision.

Chapter 6

Decorations to Display

Add a festive touch with decorations for holidays or any day.

Nature Plaque

Glue natural objects to scrap wood to create a neat nature display.

Materials

nature items, such as
small pine cones,
leaves, acorns, twigs,
and pebbles
wood, 4" x 6"
sandpaper
glue
screw-in hook
ribbon

Make Your Great Gift

1. Go outside on a nature walk and collect a variety of small nature items.*
2. Sand all rough edges of the wood.
3. Glue the nature items on the wood plaque.
4. Attach a screw-in hook to the top of the wood piece.*
5. Select a ribbon and tie it around the hook in a bow.*

Helpful Hints

- Use the tops of discarded picket fencing to create a plaque with a unique shape.
- When the plaque is finished, spray clear acrylic over the nature items to preserve them (adult only).

* May need adult help or supervision.

Decorative Tile

Make a lasting picture with a piece of clay and a toothpick.

Materials

self-hardening clay,
   neutral color
small rolling pins
toothpicks
paint
thin paintbrushes
pieces of chalk

Make Your Great Gift

1. Roll out a piece of clay to approximately 3" x 4" and ½" thick.*
2. Etch in a simple picture, such as a flower, fish, tree, or car, using a toothpick. Take care not to go all the way through the clay.*
3. Allow the clay to air dry until hard.
4. Option #1: Paint the picture using thin paintbrushes and dry.
   Option #2: Roll a piece of chalk gently over the surface, avoiding the grooves, to highlight the etched picture.

Helpful Hints

- Pre-cut the clay before beginning this activity and keep it moist in a sealed container or large plastic bag.
- Display options:*
   - Option #1—push a paperclip into back surface of rolled clay before etching on front. Hang when dry.
   - Option #2—make a hole through the top portion of the wet clay using a straw. String when dry to hang.
   - Option #3—Create a display easel by cutting a paper tube (paper towel) to approximately 1½". Cut two, ½" slits on opposite sides of the top opening. This will create a stand in which to rest the tile.

* May need adult help or supervision.

"Sun-sational" Sun Catcher

Let the sun shine through this colorful window decoration.

Materials

clear contact paper, cut
   into two 6" x 6"
   squares*
various colors of
   cellophane cut into
   small pieces
foil confetti or sequins
   in a variety of colors
   and shapes
ribbon
small wooden
   embroidery hoop

Make Your Great Gift

1. Peel the backing off of one piece of contact paper and
   position the square on the table, sticky side up. Tape to hold
   in place.*
2. Place the confetti and cellophane on the sticky side of the
   square of contact paper.
3. When the square is finished, place another square of
   contact paper over the first piece to seal in the materials.*
4. Create a frame for the sun catcher by placing it inside an
   embroidery hoop and trimming the excess contact paper
   from around the edges.*
5. Choose a color of ribbon and tie it to the top of the
   embroidery hoop to create a loop for hanging the sun
   catcher.*

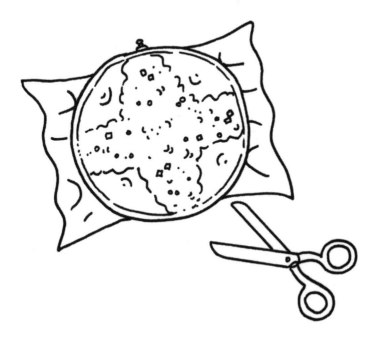

Helpful Hints

■ Use plastic margarine lids instead of embroidery hoops. Simply cut the middle from each lid to create a doughnut shape and secure the sun catcher inside the lid frame with clear tape.

■ Personalize this gift by adding a small photo to the middle of the sun catcher.

■ If cellophane is not available, use tissue paper or crepe paper instead.

Seasonal Suggestion

■ Try making a seasonal sun catcher by selecting specific shapes and colors of confetti and cellophane. Red and pink paper with sequin hearts are perfect for Valentine's Day, pastels and flower shapes are great for Mother's Day, darker colors with leaf confetti make a beautiful autumn decoration, and so on.

CD Sun Catcher

Reuse and recycle compact discs (CD) into colorful, eye-catching mobiles.

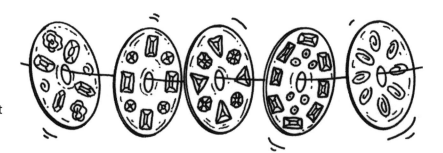

Materials

junk CD
light grit sandpaper
sequins, craft jewels,
    colorful transparent
    beads, and buttons
glue
fishing string, cut into
    approximately
    2' lengths*
paint

Make Your Great Gift

1. Lightly sand the CD on the side with the label in order to the dull surface.*
2. Paint the sanded side. Let paint dry.
3. Glue objects to the painted side. Let glue dry.
4. After the glue dries, string the CD on fishing line so that it hangs freely.
5. Give as a gift to hang in an office window or from a ceiling.

Helpful Hints

- Experiment with paint on a spare CD to check for adherence. Add a few drops of liquid dish soap to paint, if needed.
- Glue objects on mirrored side as an option.

Seasonal Suggestion

- Decorated CDs create a unique ornament for the winter holidays.

* May need adult help or supervision.

Seasonal Switch Plate Cover

Make someone's holiday merry and bright by decorating an inexpensive switch plate cover.

Materials

contact paper shapes in holiday colors or patterns

plastic switch plate cover, including screws for installation

seasonal stickers

non-toxic permanent marker

zipper-seal plastic sandwich bag

Before Beginning Cut small shapes out of the contact paper. Peel the backing off the contact paper shapes and stick them to the edge of a plastic tray.*

Make Your Great Gift

1. Decorate the switch plate cover using the stickers and contact paper shapes.
2. Place the decorated switch plate cover in a plastic zipper-seal sandwich bag, along with the screws or other hardware needed for installing the plate cover.

Seasonal Suggestion

■ Add other collage materials, such as wrapping paper and wallpaper scraps, to the switch plate cover using glue. Wrapping paper and ribbon pieces from winter holidays can add a very festive touch.

---

* May need adult help or supervision.

Fragrant Door Hanger

Nature items make a door decoration that smells as good as it looks.

Materials

nature items, such as
   leaves, flowers,
   pebbles, nuts, and
   pine needles
hole punch
zipper-seal plastic
   sandwich bag
cinnamon stick
colorful collage
   materials
ribbon

Make Your Great Gift

1. Go on a nature walk to collect small nature items.*
2. Take time to look at the materials collected and select the
    items to use for a door hanger.
3. Using the hole punch, make two holes in the sandwich bag,
    one in each of the top corners, just under
    the zipper seal.*
4. Put the nature items,
    collage materials, and
    the cinnamon stick in
    the plastic bag.
5. Thread the ribbon
    through the holes in
    the bag, creating a
    handle large enough to
    hang on a doorknob.*
6. Write a note that includes
    the following poem:

    *Here's a great-smelling
    gift with love from
    me to you
    Open it up and
    hang it on your
    door…that's all
    you have to do!*

7. Seal the sandwich bag
    and tape the note to
    the outside of the bag.

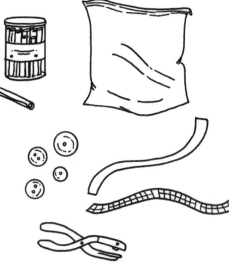

Variation

◼ Instead of a plastic bag, use a paper lunch sack. Decorate the bag with stickers, markers, or paint. Roll the sides of the sack down before making the holes and adding the handle. The extra layers of paper will keep the ribbon from ripping through the sack.*

Seasonal Suggestions

◼ Autumn is a great time to find nature items to be used for this gift. Dried leaves and nuts give the door hanger a harvest look that is perfect for fall holidays.
◼ Make this gift work for any season by using holiday collage materials such as sequins and ribbon.

Decorative Door Hanger

Make an inexpensive and personal gift out of poster board.

Materials

white poster board, cut
   into a 4" x 12"
   rectangle*
crayons
photo of child, trimmed
glue
permanent marker
clear contact paper

Before **B**eginning Cut a three-inch circle near one end of the poster board. Cut a slit from the circular hole to the closest end of the poster board. The poster board should now resemble a hotel room door hanger. Make sure this hole fits around a standard-size doorknob.*

Make Your Great Gift

1. Decorate the door hanger with crayons.
2. Glue the photo to the door hanger.
3. Use the permanent marker to write your name and the date on the back of the hanger. A special message such as "Hannah's Dad Lives Here" or "Happy Mother's Day" may be added to the front of the door hanger.*
4. Cover the door hanger with clear contact paper, trimming away the contact paper from the hole near the top.*

Helpful Hint

■ In place of clear contact paper, try laminating the door hanger. Laminating will strengthen it and give the door hanger a smooth and clear finish.*

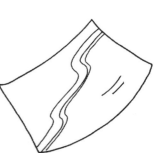

Seasonal Suggestion

■ Glue flat collage materials in holiday shapes and colors to the door hanger. Material ideas include foil confetti, wrapping paper scraps, ribbon, construction paper scraps, tissue paper scraps, and stickers.

* May need adult help or supervision.

Pictures on My Window

Create a window decoration using transparent vinyl and permanent markers.

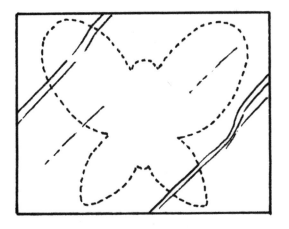

Materials

clear vinyl, cut into approximately 5" x 7" piece or smaller*
non-toxic permanent colored markers and/or paint pens
stencils
scissors

Make Your Great Gift

1. Trace a chosen shape onto the piece of vinyl using a permanent marker.*
2. Cut out the shape.*
3. Decorate the vinyl using the non-toxic permanent markers and/or paint pens. Use many colors to create a picture or design.
4. See-through pictures need to remain flat as they are wrapped and delivered. Then they are ready to shine through when stuck to a window, mirror, or refrigerator.

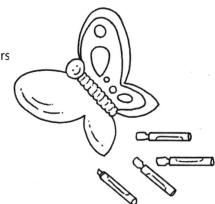

Helpful Hints

■ Vinyl can be found in fabric and department stores by the yard.
■ Substitute transparent colored vinyl for clear vinyl.

Seasonal Suggestions

■ Designs, shapes, and colors can be modified for many different holidays and gift-giving occasions.
■ A picture drawn on a simple square piece of vinyl would be a treasure for a grandparent on Grandparent's Day.

* May need adult help or supervision.

Colorful Wall Hanging

Create a unique and long-lasting picture using fabric, an embroidery hoop, and oil pastels.

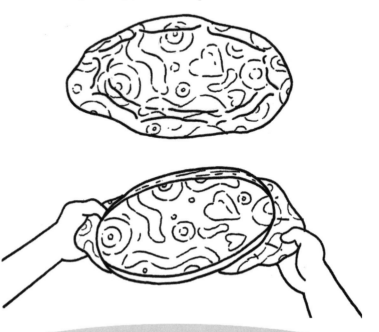

Materials

muslin fabric or other
    cotton fabric (beige
    or white)
scissors
non-toxic oil pastels
food coloring
water
paintbrushes
embroidery hoops
string or yarn
ribbon

Before Beginning Pre-cut fabric in a circle, two inches wider than the embroidery hoop purchased. Put a few drops of food coloring into a bowl of water for each color used.*

Make Your Great Gift

1. Draw a picture or design on the fabric using oil pastels.
2. Paint over the top of the picture using the food coloring/water mixture.
3. Allow fabric to dry.
4. Place the fabric over the inner hoop. Secure the outer hoop over fabric. Tighten and pull until fabric is taut.*
5. Trim excess fabric from edges.*
6. Loop a string through the tightening screw and tie to form hanger.
7. If desired cover the screw with a ribbon bow by gluing or tying it on.

Helpful Hints

- Test oil pastels on fabric before using to be sure they will adhere to the fabric.
- Substitute oil pastels with bold colors of watercolor paint. It will create a tie-dye effect. Detail can be added with non-toxic permanent markers.
- Paint the outer portion of the embroidery hoop using the food coloring/water mixture or watercolors.*
- Pictures drawn on thin fabric and placed in small hoops can be hung in the window. The drawing will stand out as the sun shines through.
- Add a little diluted glitter paint over the top of the picture instead of food coloring/water mixture.

Seasonal Suggestion

- The smallest hoops can be used to create ornaments for winter holidays.

* May need adult help or supervision.

"Happy Holidays" Wreath

This wreath will be the perfect addition to any holiday décor.

Materials

cardboard or poster
   board cut into a 12"
   donut shape*
seasonal collage
   materials
glue
ribbon
tape

Make Your Great Gift

1. Write a holiday greeting on the back of the wreath. Include your name and the date.*
2. Glue seasonal collage materials on the front of the cardboard wreath shape.
3. After the wreath dries, tie a bow using wide ribbon and attach it to the front of the wreath.*
4. Create a loop using thin ribbon and secure it with tape to the back of the top of the wreath. This will enable the recipient to hang the wreath.*

Seasonal Suggestions

■ Try the following seasonal ideas:
  ■ For spring holidays: pastel ribbon, pastel tissue paper, dried flowers, Easter grass, and wallpaper scraps.
  ■ For fall holidays: dried leaves, acorns, seeds, raffia, small squares cut from sandpaper and brown paper sacks, deep colors of tissue paper and construction paper.
  ■ For winter holidays: shredded Mylar, pine cones, pine branches, jingle bells, metallic ribbon, foil, wrapping paper scraps, bows, and cotton balls.
■ When making a wreath for a family occasion, such as a family member's birthday, put a photo of that family member on the front of the wreath.

* May need adult help or supervision.

Table Wreath

Make this wreath the center of attention at a holiday gathering.

Materials

Styrofoam scraps or
   floral foam, cut into
   approximately 1½" x
   4" x 4" pieces or
   larger if necessary*
evergreen twigs
dried flowers
round beads
small pine cones
glue

Make Your Great Gift

1. Push pieces of evergreen and dried flowers into the Styrofoam. Fill in the space around the sides and top edge of the Styrofoam and leave an unobstructed area in the center.
2. Push pine cones into the evergreen and flowers.
3. Glue beads and other decorations randomly around the wreath.

Helpful Hints

- Twist pipe cleaners around a pencil and push into Styrofoam. Slide on a couple of beads.*
- Cut pieces of wire garland to twist and push into Styrofoam.*
- Glue unscented potpourri pieces directly onto Styrofoam.
- Experiment making dried flowers by hanging small flowers with long stems upside down in a sunny area.

Seasonal Suggestion

- Create an autumn wreath for Thanksgiving using bits of straw, acorns, pine cones, dried leaves, dried wheat, and other appropriate materials glued onto Styrofoam.

* May need adult help or supervision.

Painted Candle

Use paint to add refreshing color to a plain candle.

Materials

votive size or other
   small, thick candles
fine sandpaper, cut into
   small pieces
tempera or acrylic
   paint, slightly thick
thin paintbrushes
netting or tissue paper,
   cut in approximately
   8" squares*
yarn, cut into 8" pieces*

Make Your Great Gift

1. Lightly sand the sides of
   the candle. When finished,
   there should be slight scratches on the
   surface of the wax.
2. Paint the sides of the candles using various simple designs
   and shapes, such as dots, stripes, circles, and so on.
3. After the paint dries, wrap the candle in a square piece of
   netting or tissue paper and tie with yarn.*

Helpful Hints

■ Paint should be thick enough that it does not run when
   brushed on the candle.
■ If paint bubbles on candle, repeat sanding step.

Beaded Candle

Add charm to a plain candle with beaded studs.

Materials

small candles
beaded studs (metal or
    rhinestone)
small plastic hammers

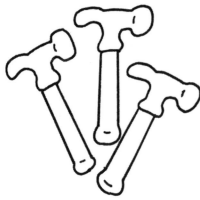

Make Your Great Gift

1. Push the beaded studs into the sides of the candle. Cover all sides, avoiding the top and bottom of the candle.*
2. Use plastic hammers to drive in studs as needed. The tips of the studs are sharp, so use extra caution.*

Helpful Hints

■ Use the beaded studs to make a pattern on the candle.*
■ Add discarded small pierced earrings to the designs.

Seasonal Suggestion

■ This gift idea can be used for a variety of gift-giving occasions. A red candle with heart-shaped studs could be a gift for Valentine's Day, or a thick taper candle with small studs could be used as part of a wreath created for a fall or winter occasion.

* May need adult help or supervision.

Colorful Candle

Enhance ordinary candles with melted crayons.

Materials

candles, solid color
warming tray*
old muffin tin
long cotton swabs
old crayons

Make Your Great Gift

1. Remove paper from old crayons and sort them by color.
2. Sort crayons into a muffin tin.
3. Place the muffin tin on the warming tray. Plug in and heat to liquefy the crayons (adult only).
4. Use cotton swabs to decorate the candle by dipping the swabs into melted crayon, and then brushing them quickly on the candle.*

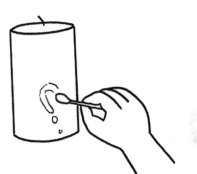

Helpful Hints

■ Before using the warming tray, discuss safety precautions: Avoid touching the warming tray, muffin tin, and liquid crayons.*
■ Crayon melters can be used instead of a muffin tin and warming tray.
■ Put paper muffin liners in the muffin tin before melting crayons to make cleanup easier.
■ Put decorated candle in homemade Stained Glass Candleholder (see page 118).

Seasonal Suggestions

■ Use glitter crayons to decorate candles for winter holidays.
■ Create a Thanksgiving centerpiece candle using browns, berry colors, and other dark colored crayons.

* May need adult help or supervision.

Stained Glass Candleholder

Create a candleholder using a small glass jar, liquid starch, and tissue paper.

Materials

colored crepe paper or
    streamers
scissors
small glass jar, such as a
    baby food jar
liquid starch
paintbrushes
aluminum foil or
    plastic tray
zipper-seal plastic
    sandwich bags
    (optional)
glitter (optional)
scrap wire ribbon or
    wire garland

Make Your Great Gift

1. Tear or cut crepe paper into small pieces.
2. Paint liquid starch onto the jar, stick on crepe paper, and then apply another coat of starch over the top to adhere loose ends.*
3. Overlap the crepe paper over the sides of the jar to cover it completely.
4. Place the jar on a non-paper surface, such as aluminum foil or a plastic tray, to dry. Or, after drying slightly, place the jar in a closed sandwich bag containing glitter and roll it gently on the floor. Remove to dry.
5. Wrap ribbon or garland around the top rim of the jar.

Helpful Hints

- Watered-down white glue can be substituted for liquid starch.
- Save tissue paper from gifts to use in this project as a substitute for crepe paper.
- Drop in a votive candle, such as one made in the Colorful Candles activity (page 117) to complete this luminescent gift.

Seasonal Suggestion

- Obtain printed tissue paper or crepe paper that corresponds with the gift-giving occasion. For example, a cake and party print for a birthday; cars or sports imprint for Father's Day; red, white, and blue for Fourth of July; or a black and orange pumpkin print for Halloween.

* May need adult help or supervision.

Beaded Ornament

Put small fingers to work producing colorful decorations with pipe cleaners and beads.

Materials

beads with large holes, colored/transparent
pipe cleaners
small suction cups with hooks

Make Your Great Gift

1. Secure one end of the pipe cleaner by bending it slightly to prevent the beads from sliding off.
2. Slide beads onto the straight end of the pipe cleaner.
3. Create patterns using alternate colors. Secure the end by bending it in slightly when finished.*
4. Attach the ends of the pipe cleaner together to form a circle. Then twist and bend the circle together to form a colorful sculpture.*
5. Hang the beaded sculpture on a suction hook and place in a window.

Helpful Hint

■ Make two or more strings of beads, form them into circles, and twist them together to create a variety of shapes.*

Seasonal Suggestion

■ Use colored beads and shapes that correspond to a holiday to vary the gift-giving opportunities. For example, use white, pink, and red beads for Valentines Day, or pretty pastels for Mother's Day.

* May need adult help or supervision.

Bottle Decoration

Create an ornamental gift worth hanging, using a plastic bottle and paint.

Materials

small, clear plastic
   water bottle,
   approximately 8 oz.
tempera paint
plastic spoons
tape
ribbon or yarn

Make Your Great Gift

1. Spoon the paint into the plastic bottle.*
2. Experiment creating new colors by mixing two or more together inside the bottle.
3. Close the bottle with a lid and secure with tape.
4. Shake the container to coat the inside completely. Rolling the bottles around on the floor also works.
5. Remove the tape and the lid. Pour out any extra paint.*
6. Allow the bottle to air dry completely with lid off, in a warm location. Turn occasionally to move paint around that might have settled to the bottom.
7. When paint feels dry to the touch, place the lid back on the bottle.
8. Tie a piece of yarn or ribbon around the neck of the bottle to hang the ornament.*
9. Decorate neck portion of the bottle by attaching a ribbon bow.

Helpful Hints

■ Try using glitter paint for an interesting effect.

■ Use wire-enforced ribbon to create a decorative bow.

■ Ready-made clear plastic ornaments or snack containers can be substituted for the bottle.

■ Substitute acrylic paints for tempera paint.*

■ Test tempera paint for adherence. If it cracks when dry, add a few drops of dish soap to liquid paint.

Seasonal Suggestion

■ Several bottles strung together can make a unique party decoration for such occasions as Christmas, Fourth of July, or a birthday.

* May need adult help or supervision.

Cinnamon Family

Give a sweet-smelling and eye-pleasing gift!

Materials

ground cinnamon, 8 oz. or more*

flour, 8 oz.*

water, 6-8 oz.*

mixing bowl

rolling pins*

cookie cutters, people shape

wax paper or cooling racks*

white paint

toothpicks or cotton swabs

drinking straws

thin ribbon or string

 Before Beginning Pour cinnamon in a bowl to prevent dust from spreading to the eyes. Supervise closely as cinnamon can irritate the eyes and skin.*

Make Your Great Gift

1. Add flour to cinnamon and mix.*
2. Gradually add the water, starting with approximately four ounces. Stir the mix.*
3. Add the remaining water until a smooth, dough ball forms. (You may not need all 8 ounces.)*
4. Sprinkle a little cinnamon on a piece of wax paper and place all or a small portion of the dough on top.*
5. Sprinkle more cinnamon on top, particularly if the dough is sticky. Cover with another layer of wax paper.*
6. Flatten dough to approximately ½" thick using a rolling pin. If dough is still sticky, sprinkle on more cinnamon and roll again.*
7. Remove the top layer of wax paper. Cut out the shapes using people cookie cutters.*
8. Place a hole in top of each cinnamon person using a toothpick or end of a drinking straw.*
9. Allow cinnamon people to air dry on wax paper or on cooling racks. It may take 24 to 48 hours.

* May need adult help or supervision.

10. After cinnamon people dry, use a toothpick or cotton swab dipped in white paint to create features by using dots, lines, and squiggles.
11. Thread string or ribbon through each cinnamon person and tie. They can be strung individually or together as a "family" on one long piece of ribbon.*

Helpful Hints

■ Wash thoroughly after handling dough to avoid skin irritation.
■ Use other colors of paint to add features to the people shapes.

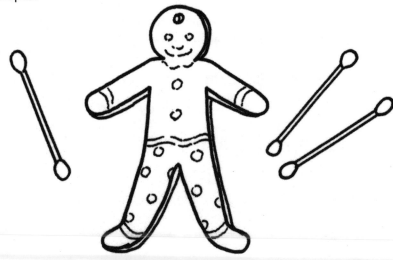

* May need adult help or supervision.

Jazzy Jigsaw Pin

Create a lovely pin created with tagboard, bar pin, and paint.

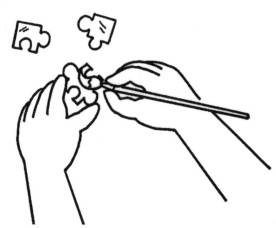

Materials

small cardboard jigsaw
   pieces (purchased or
   from old puzzles)
tagboard or heavy
   poster board, cut
   into small shapes*
glue
thin paintbrushes
paint
glitter
zipper-seal plastic
   sandwich bags
bar pins

Make Your Great Gift

1. Choose several jigsaw puzzle pieces.
2. Paint the cardboard or unprinted side of the puzzle pieces.
3. After the paint dries, glue the puzzle pieces on a tagboard shape in a unique design. Let dry.
4. If desired, apply a thin layer of glue over parts of the painted pin. Drop the pin into a zipper-seal sandwich bag containing glitter. Seal and shake. Let dry.
5. When pin is completely dry, secure the bar pin to the back. If it's not a self-adhesive pin, use glue to secure it.*

Helpful Hint

■ Add or substitute colored toothpicks, small wooden shapes, cut drinking straws, or beads as pin decorations.

Seasonal Suggestions

■ Cut out tagboard backing into shapes to reflect various holidays or special occasions. For example, cut out a tree, snowflake, or star for winter holidays.
■ Cut several tagboard pieces in the shape of a turkey; decorate with Indian corn kernels or pinecones as described above. Instead of making a pin, attach the tagboard turkeys to rectangle-shaped pieces of tagboard to use as place cards for Thanksgiving. Make as many as needed.

* May need adult help or supervision.

Chapter 7

Say It with a Card

Create unique cards and stationery.

A "Hand-y" Card

Trace a child's hand to create a quick, easy note card.

Materials

construction paper,
  9" x 12" sheet
crayons or markers
scissors

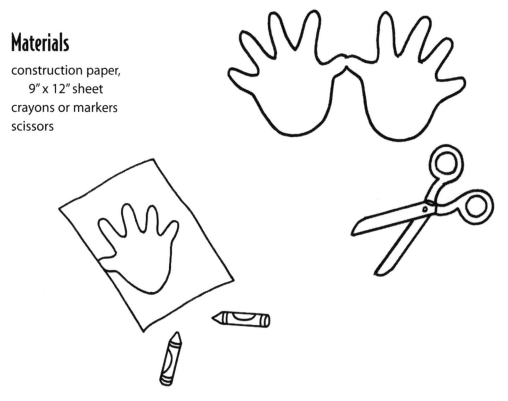

Make Your Great Gift

1. Fold the construction paper in half to create a 9" x 6" rectangle card.*
2. Place your hand on the paper, with the thumb positioned next to the fold in the paper.
3. Trace around your hand using a crayon or a marker.*
4. Cut out the hand shape, leaving the fold along the outside of the thumb intact.*
5. Decorate the hand-shaped card with crayons and markers.
6. Write a short message inside the card to the recipient.*

* May need adult help or supervision.

Painted Postcards

Use watercolors and cardstock to create simple postcards that are almost too pretty to use.

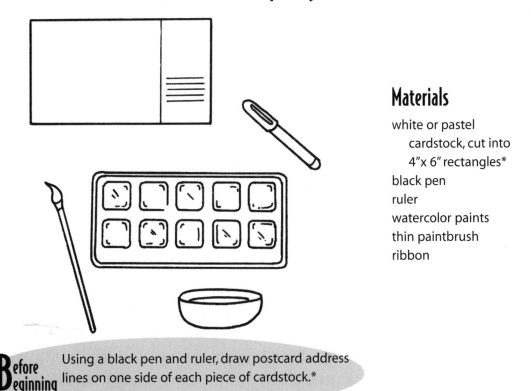

Materials

white or pastel
 cardstock, cut into
 4"x 6" rectangles*
black pen
ruler
watercolor paints
thin paintbrush
ribbon

Before Beginning Using a black pen and ruler, draw postcard address lines on one side of each piece of cardstock.*

Make Your Great Gift

1. Paint each card on the side without the lines.
2. After they dry, stack the cards and tie a ribbon around them.*

Helpful Hint

■ If possible, use the address lines on a commercial-made postcard as a master copy, then run each piece of cardstock through the copy machine.*

Seasonal Suggestion

■ Make seasonal shapes from construction paper, such as a leaf shape for Thanksgiving. Write a holiday greeting to the recipient of the postcards on the seasonal shape and slip the note under the tied ribbon.

* May need adult help or supervision.

Foil Etched Card

Create a card worth framing with paint and foil wrapping paper.

Materials

foil wrapping paper, cut
   into 3 $\frac{1}{2}$" x 4 $\frac{1}{2}$"
   pieces*
paint, with several
   drops of dish soap
thin paintbrushes
construction paper or
   cardstock
markers
glue
foil ribbon, cut into
   small pieces
foil star stickers

Make Your Great Gift

1. Paint a solid section in the middle of the piece of foil
    wrapping paper, leaving a border of the paper free from
    paint.*
2. Let the painted area sit for a couple of minutes.
3. Using the handle end of a paintbrush, etch a design or
    drawing into the painted area, revealing the foil surface
    underneath.
4. While the paint is drying, fold a half piece of construction
    paper once to create a card.
5. Write messages and decorate the inside of the card using
    markers.*
6. When the paint is dry, glue the foil wrapping paper to the
    outside front cover of the construction paper card.*
7. Create a border around the edge of the card using foil star
    stickers and ribbon scraps.

Helpful Hints

■ Use scrap foil wrapping paper left over from holidays instead of purchasing a full roll.

■ If the paint produces bubbles on the paper surface, add a few drops of dish soap to the print to help it adhere.

■ Glue a bow or sequins to the front of the card as a substitution for a border decoration.

Seasonal Suggestions

■ This card is a great activity for winter holidays. Etch symbols related to the season, such as bells, stars, trees, and snowflakes. *

■ Create a Valentine by using red foil paper cut in a heart shape or etching a heart into white or pink paint.

Lacing Card

Construct a lively card with paper, fabric scraps, and poster board.

Materials

construction paper, cut
  into desired shape
  approximately
  5"x 7"*
hole punch
poster board, cut into
  desired shape
  approximately
  5"x 7"*
stencils
variety of scraps, such
  as thin paper ribbon
  scraps, fabric ribbon
  scraps, colored
  lacing string used for
  beadwork and,
  yarn scraps
markers
tape

Before **B**eginning Choose a shape to use for the card, such as a circle or free-form shaped flower (see seasonal suggestions on the following page). Cut out the shape from the poster board. Cut out the same shape from a piece of construction paper. Save this for the card back.*

Make Your Great Gift

1. Use a hole punch to put holes around the outer edge of the card.*
2. Lace a variety of scrap materials in and out of the holes. Experiment by crossing over the card to create a web-like appearance. Secure ends with tape. Lay aside.
3. Write messages and draw pictures using markers on the construction paper shape.*
4. Attach the laced top to the construction paper back by punching a matching hole through both in the upper left corner and tying together with scrap ribbon or yarn.*

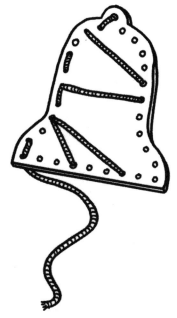

Helpful Hints

- Pipe cleaners or plastic coated wire are good for begining lacers.
- Substitute cardstock for poster board.
- Wrap tape around the sewing end of yarn or ribbon, creating a "needle," to aid in lacing.*
- Encourage children to cut out their own shapes.

Seasonal Suggestions

- Shapes that could be used include hearts for Valentine's Day, a car for Father's Day, and stars or trees for winter holidays. Corresponding colors of poster board and scraps to a holiday also lends this activity to many card-giving occasions.

* May need adult help or supervision.

Polka Dot Frame Card

Use pencils and paint to decorate this keepsake card.

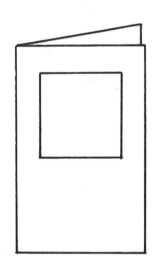

Materials

white or pastel
  cardstock, 8½" x 11"
  sheet
shallow plastic
  containers
sponges
unsharpened pencils
  with erasers
photo of child, at least
  3½" x 5" in size
tape
pen
paint, various colors

Before beginning Prepare the frame cards by folding the cardstock in half to create 8½" x 5½" cards. Cut a 3½" x 3½" square or circle in the center of the front of the card.*

Make Your Great Gift

1. Place a sponge inside each shallow container and pour in a small amount of paint. Place one pencil, eraser side down in each container.*
2. Use the eraser ends of the pencils and paint to print dots on the front and back of the cardstock.
3. After the paint dries, tape the photo on the inside of the card, positioning the picture so that it shows through the frame in the front of the card.*
4. Write a special message for the intended recipient on the inside of the card.*

Helpful Hints

- If cardstock is not readily available, use construction paper or poster board instead.
- Washable inkpads make a wonderful, mess-free substitute for the paint in this activity.

* May need adult help or supervision.

Old Clothes Patch Card

Turn old clothing into a colorful card and a conversation piece.

Materials

old patterned shirts, old
ties or scarves,
rickrack, ribbon, and
other fabric scraps,
cut into small shapes
or pieces
construction paper
glue
colored pencils or
markers

Make Your Great Gift

1. Fold a piece of construction paper in half to form an
   8 ½" x 5 ½" piece.*
2. Glue fabric scraps to the front of the card to form a design.
3. Create borders and accents by gluing on other fabric scraps.
4. After the card dries, write a greeting inside.*

Helpful Hints

■ Substitute cardstock for construction paper to create a
  sturdier card.
■ Cut scraps with serrated scissors.
■ Add small buttons for variety.

Seasonal Suggestion

■ For a Father's Day gift, reuse shirt pockets by cutting them
  off and gluing them to a card and decorating them. Slide an
  index card containing a special message into the pocket .

* May need adult help or supervision.

Peek-a-Boo Card

Make a special card with a surprise message.

Materials

construction paper, cut
  into a 9" x 6" heart
  shape*
small construction
  paper scraps
glue
construction paper, cut
  into a 2½" x 2½"
  heart shape*
scissors
craft stick
pen

Make Your Great Gift

1. Decorate the larger heart shape using glue and small construction paper scraps.
2. After the glue dries, cut a three-inch horizontal slit in the middle of the heart.*
3. Write a short phrase, such as "I love you," to the recipient of the card. Write the message on one side of the smaller heart shape.*
4. Glue the small heart to the end of a craft stick, with the message facing away from the stick.
5. When the glue dries, the small heart on the craft stick can be placed through the slit in the larger heart. As the craft stick moves up and down, the message on the smaller heart will appear and disappear, playing peek-a-boo with the recipient.*

Helpful Hints

■ Use other lightweight collage materials, such as wrapping paper scraps, sequins, or craft foam shapes.

■ Use small amounts of glue to keep from weighing down the card.

■ A thicker cardstock paper or even poster board may be used in place of the construction paper to create a sturdier card.

Seasonal Suggestions

■ This heart-shaped card is an obvious choice for Valentine's Day. Choosing different messages such as "Happy Father's Day" can also make this card appropriate for other occasions.

■ Change the shape of the card to be used for other holidays. Try decorating a balloon shape and adding a message of "Happy Birthday!"

* May need adult help or supervision.

Handprint Blossoms

Produce a flower card that is unique and memorable using a handprint, pipe cleaner, and tissue paper.

Materials

paint
shallow plates or trays
white construction
    paper
scissors
green pipe cleaners
transparent tape
green tissue paper
    sheets, cut into
    approximately
    5" squares*

Make Your Great Gift

1. Place hands on a plate or tray containing a small amount of paint. Create several handprints on the piece of white construction paper.
2. After the paint dries, cut out the handprints.*
3. Attach a green pipe cleaner stem to each handprint using transparent tape.
4. Cut and tape tissue paper or wrap it around the pipe cleaner to form the leaves.*
5. Messages and pictures can be put on the back of the handprint flower using colored pencils or markers.*
6. Tie to a package or insert in a gift bag for someone special.

Helpful Hints

■ Create a bunch of flowers to put in a decorated pot or give as a bouquet.
■ Use green construction paper scraps instead of tissue paper to make leaves.

* May need adult help or supervision.

Handprint Stationery

Family members will treasure this notepaper depicting a child's handprints.

Materials

white copier paper
washable inkpads, dark
   colors
black marker
colored copier paper
copy machine
ribbon

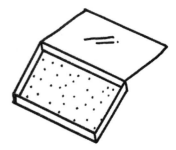

Make Your Great Gift

1. Make hand and fingerprints all over the piece of white paper using a washable inkpad.
2. Write the name or title of the recipient of the gift across the top of the paper using a black marker. For example, "From the desk of Nick's Mom" or "Grandpa's Notes."*
3. Set the copy machine to a light setting and place colored paper in the copier. Make at least five copies of the paper. The final product should still show the hand and finger prints, but only as a faded background on the paper. The title across the top of the page should still be clearly visible.*
4. Tie each set of stationery together with ribbon.*

* May need adult help or supervision.

Stamped Stationery

Make simple notepaper using ink stamps.

Materials

white copier paper
washable inkpads,
   several colors
small seasonal ink
   stamps
ribbon

Make Your Great Gift

1. Decorate the edges of six pieces of paper using the ink and ink stamps.
2. Gently tie a ribbon around five pieces of the stationery.*
3. Write a note to the recipient of the gift on the sixth piece of stationery. Fold this note in thirds and slide it under the ribbon around the stack of note paper.*

Helpful Hint

■ Place a 7½" x 10" piece of paper in the center of each 8½" x 11" piece of copy paper. This provides a frame to decorate and protect the middle of the paper from stray ink stamp marks.*

Seasonal Suggestions

■ Make festive winter holiday stationery using metallic color inkpads such as gold or silver.
■ Make your own seasonal ink stamps by gluing small craft foam shapes to the bottoms of empty film canisters.

* May need adult help or supervision.

Swirl Card

A shiny card created with corn syrup and food coloring is a delight to the eyes.

Materials

light corn syrup
shallow pan (e.g. pie tin, cake pan)
food coloring
eyedroppers
white construction paper, 8 ½" x 11"
container to catch syrup drippings
markers

Before **B**eginning Pour corn syrup into the pan until it is approximately one inch deep.*

Make Your Great Gift

1. Drop food coloring onto corn syrup, using eyedroppers if necessary. Use a variety of colors.
2. Place construction paper on top of corn syrup and food coloring mixture, then carefully lift up allowing excess to drip off.*
3. Hang the paper to drip over a container.
4. Let dry for 24 to 48 hours.
5. Fold paper in half to create a card.
6. Write messages and draw pictures inside the card.*

Helpful Hints

■ To conserve corn syrup, use a small amount in a small bread pan and cut paper to fit.
■ To remove excess corn syrup quickly, run construction paper under water for a few seconds after dipping in mixture. This will also cause colors to "swirl" together more.*
■ Sprinkling salt on a slightly dry picture will absorb some of the sticky texture and give it a crystal-like appearance.

Seasonal Suggestion

■ Cut paper into heart shapes and sprinkle on heart-shaped tissue paper or confetti after dipping into corn syrup and food coloring mixture for a special Valentine card.*

* May need adult help or supervision.

Woven Card

Construct a cheerful card by weaving with items such as ribbon, wrapping paper, and crepe paper.

Materials

construction paper,
  8½" x 11"
scissors
ribbon scraps, cut 12"
  long*
wrapping paper scraps,
  cut into strips of
  various widths and
  12" long; crepe
  paper streamers, cut
  12" long; paper
  ribbon scraps, cut
  12" long*
tape
white paper, cut into
  8" x 11" pieces or
  smaller*
colored markers
glue

Make Your Great Gift

1. Fold the piece of construction paper in half lengthwise to create an 8½" x 5½" card.*
2. Cut slits into construction paper, beginning on the folded edge and stopping about an inch from the outer edge. Cut wavy lines in addition to straight ones. Open the paper.*
3. Weave scraps over and under slits in the paper, alternating starting point to create a weaving pattern. Tape strips on both ends.
4. Draw pictures and write messages on the piece of white paper. Glue this to the inside of the woven card.*
5. After the glue dries, fold along the width of the paper to form an elaborate card for someone special.

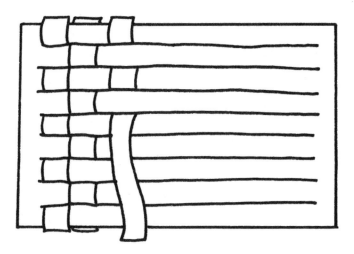

Helpful Hints

■ Create this card over several days.

■ Pre-draw lines to follow when cutting construction paper. Or, cut slits in construction paper before the beginning activity.*

■ Cut wrapping paper using serrated scissors or cut smooth wavy lines instead of straight.

Seasonal Suggestion

■ Use printed wrapping paper scraps and other scraps that correspond to a particular holiday, such as balloons for birthdays or foil paper for winter holidays.

Chapter 8

Wrap It Up!

Create a variety of papers, bags, boxes, and baskets for wrapping child-made gifts.

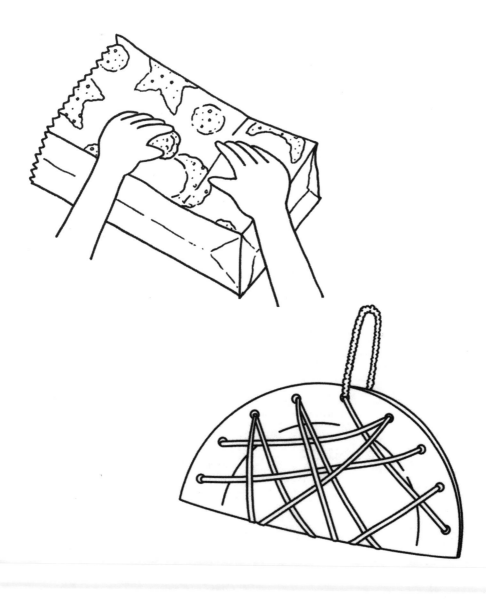

Bubble Wrap Paper

Create an interesting wrapping paper using bubble wrap and paint.

Materials

bubble wrap packing
    material
tape
paint, with a few drops
    of dish soap added
thick paintbrush or
    sponge paintbrush
newsprint, bulletin
    board paper, or
    other lightweight
    paper

Make Your Great Gift

1. Lay bubble wrap on trays or table surface. Tape corners of bubble wrap to the table.*
2. Paint the bubble wrap using a variety of colors.
3. Lay a piece of paper over the painted area. Rub the entire paper area in order to transfer the print.
4. Lift up paper carefully and allow it to dry.
5. Use the paper to wrap a homemade gift!

Helpful Hints

- After the bubble wrap print has dried, use markers or crayons to add features and pictures to the print.
- Use various sizes of bubble wrap to create interesting designs.

Seasonal Suggestion

- Color variations lend this activity to a variety of special occasions, for example, pastel colors for spring holidays or glitter paint for winter holidays.

* May need adult help or supervision.

Bubble Blowing Wrapping Paper

Combine bubbles and food coloring to make a lovely wrapping paper.

Materials

cake pans, 9" x 13", or
    jellyroll pans
water
liquid dish soap
food coloring
white butcher paper, cut
    into large pieces*
drinking straws
newspaper
crayons or non-toxic oil
    pastels

Before Beginning Cover work surface with newspaper. Fill pans with water about half full. Drop in food coloring, creating one color for each pan. Add several drops of liquid dish soap. Test solution by placing one end of the straw in mixture, and blowing through the other end. Bubbles should appear over the top of the pans. If not, add more soap.*

Make Your Great Gift

1. Use a straw and piece of butcher paper. Practice blowing out of the straw. When ready, blow into colored soap solution.
2. When the bubbles rise above the mixture, lay the paper carefully over the top to "catch" the color.*
3. Repeat the procedure for the other colors, if desired.
4. Allow the paper to dry.
5. Use crayons or non-toxic oil pastels to add designs or create pictures out of bubble prints. When finished, it is ready to wrap up a homemade wonder.

Helpful Hints

- Put a hole near the top of each straw using a straight pin to prevent soap mixture from being sucked up into the mouth.*
- Use an animal-shaped sponge and paint instead of crayons or oil pastels.

Salty Wrapping Paper Sensation

Create a simple, eye-catching wrapping paper with glue, cookie cutters, and salt.

Materials

cookie cutters
glue, in a shallow pan or
     plate
butcher paper, colored,
     cut in large pieces*
salt, in a bowl
plastic spoon

Make Your Great Gift

1. Dip the cookie cutter into glue. Tap it lightly on pan edge to remove excess glue.
2. Place the cookie cutter onto butcher paper, creating a glue print.
3. Use a variety of cookie cutters and cover the paper with prints.
4. Sprinkle the salt, using a spoon, on glue prints. Move the paper around to disperse and pour off extra salt.
5. After glue dries, the paper is ready to use!

Helpful Hint

■ Pour salt into saltshakers, empty candy sprinkle containers, or glitter containers. Cover some of the holes with tape to control the amount of salt released.*

Seasonal Suggestion

■ For winter holidays, try doing this activity on plain foil wrapping paper to add a little sparkle.

* May need adult help or supervision.

Wrapping Paper Bonanza

Use paint and almost anything else to create fun and fancy wrapping paper.

Before Beginning Place the paint in shallow dishes or trays.*

Materials

paint
shallow containers
seasonal items for
    printing
large sheet of butcher
    paper or newsprint
clear tape

Make Your Great Gift

1. Dip the seasonal objects in the paint and make prints on the butcher paper.
2. After the paper dries, use it to wrap a gift. Secure the edges with clear tape.

Helpful Hints

- Use this same technique with large sheets of bulletin board paper to create tablecloths. Use paint and seasonal sponge shapes or cookie cutters to create a table covering for a holiday event.
- Before beginning this activity, select a large area where the wrapping paper can be set while it dries.
- Matching cards can be made using the same materials and a folded piece of construction paper.

Seasonal Suggestions

- Sponge shapes and cookie cutters come in a wide variety of holiday characters and shapes and are easy to handle while making prints on the paper. Consider other seasonal items as well:
  - Autumn holidays: leaves, feathers, nature objects
  - Winter holidays: plastic ornaments, pine branches, heart-shaped candy boxes
  - Spring holidays: plastic eggs, flowers, kite string
  - Summer holidays: foam balls, seashells, feet

* May need adult help or supervision.

Tape Print Gift Bag

Have fun while creating a unique gift bag with masking tape and paint.

Materials

masking tape, variety of
   widths
paint
paper bag, grocery or
   lunch sack
scissors
thick paintbrushes

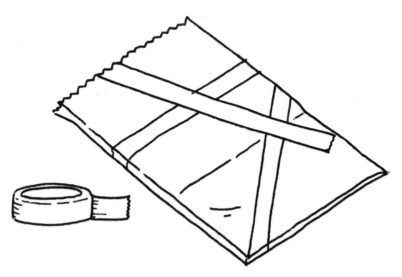

Make Your Great Gift

1. Tear off or cut strips of masking tape. Create a flat design by placing the tape on the bag.
2. Completely cover the taped area with paint. Try using a variety of colors in stripes or swirls.
3. After the bag dries, pull off the tape.*
4. Repeat steps 1-3 on the other side of the bag, if desired.
5. Place homemade gift inside and cover with piece of coordinating tissue paper!

* May need adult help or supervision.

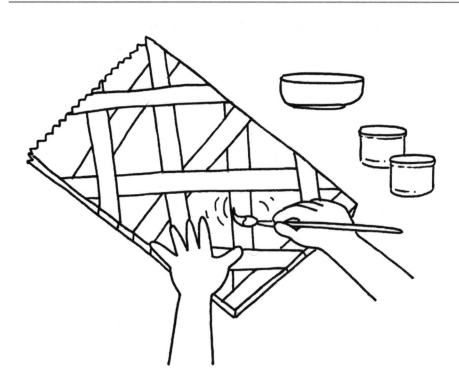

Helpful Hints

- Precut the tape and stick it to a tray where it can be easily removed to use.*
- Gently rub dry brushes or toothbrushes across the tape to loosen edges and remove the tape.*
- Fasten shut by punching holes through the top and tying with a piece of yarn or ribbon.*

Seasonal Suggestions

- Create star or snowflake patterns for winter holidays by crossing several pieces of tape at a center point. Add a glittery effect by sprinkling on salt while white or silver paint is wet.*
- For spring holidays, create a flower using the crossing pattern, and paint with pastel colors. After tape is removed, place pastel colored sticker dots in the center of crossed areas to make flower center.

* May need adult help or supervision.

"My Feet" Gift Bag

Make a personal gift bag by tracing your foot!

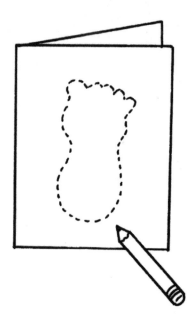

Materials

white construction
    paper, 9" x 12" sheet
pencil
watercolor paint
thin paintbrush
yarn
scissors

Make Your Great Gift

1. Fold the construction paper in half.
2. Using a pencil, trace your right foot onto one side of the folded construction paper.*
3. Cut the foot shape out of the folded paper, creating two identical foot shapes.*
4. Use watercolor paint to decorate one side of each of the foot shapes.
5. Place the two shapes back to back, with the painted sides facing out.
6. Tape or staple the sides and bottom of the foot shapes together, creating a small bag. Be sure to leave the top of the foot shapes open.*
7. Punch a hole in the top of each foot shape and string yarn through the holes to create a handle for the bag.*

Helpful Hint

■ Turn this gift sack into the gift! Write a short note to the
recipient of the gift. Across the top of the note write, "I think
you are toe-tally great!" Roll up the note and place it inside
the gift bag.*

Seasonal Suggestion

■ This sweet gift sack is the perfect size for displaying
homemade flowers. Try using it with the homemade flowers
on pages 28-30.

Sponging Gift Bag

Liven up a plain brown bag for gift giving by using sponges and paint.

Materials

brown paper bag
newspaper or plastic
    grocery bags
sponges, cut into varied
    shapes*
paint
salt

Make Your Great Gift

1. Stuff the brown paper bag with newspapers or plastic bags to add support when painting both sides.
2. Use sponges dipped in paint to cover the outer sides of the bag. Use various colors of paint. (Overlapping creates new colors!)
3. While sponged paint is wet, sprinkle on salt. Shake off excess salt.
4. Dry completely. The bag is ready to hold a special gift!

Helpful Hints

■ Experiment with other things to use as painting tools, such as wadded up newspaper or plastic grocery bags.
■ Create matching gift cards by sponge painting on one side of a 3" x 5" piece of poster board or index card.

Seasonal Suggestions

■ When using specific colors such as red and green for Christmas, let one color dry before using the next.
■ Add some white "snow" paint sprinkled with salt.

* May need adult help or supervision.

"Wrap it Up" Canister

Wrap up a special piece of artwork using a potato chip can.

Materials

potato chip can, clean
  and empty
construction paper
toothbrush
paint
crayons or markers
ribbon
glue or clear tape
a drawing done by
  child

Before **B**eginning Cut the construction paper so that it will fit around the potato chip can.*

Make Your Great Gift

1. Dip the toothbrush in the paint, then run your thumb across the bristles to splatter paint on the construction paper.
2. While the paint is drying, use crayons or markers and another piece of construction paper to make a picture for the recipient of the gift.
3. When the paint is dry, wrap the paper around the can and secure it with glue or clear tape.*
4. Roll up the picture and place it inside the can.
5. Tie a ribbon around the can.*

Helpful Hint

■ Use a cardboard wrapping paper tube instead of the can. Cut the tube in half and cover it with the decorated paper. Tape one end closed. Place a picture inside, and then secure the other end with a small piece of wrapping or construction paper and a rubber band.*

Seasonal Suggestion

■ Change the canister to suit the holiday. Vary the color of the paper and paint used and consider adding flat collage materials to the outside of the canister.

* May need adult help or supervision.

Decorative Gift Box

Recycle and rejuvenate small boxes with paint, sequins, and stickers.

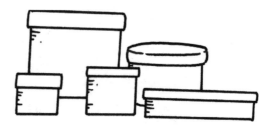

Materials

small boxes with lids,
  such as checkbook
  boxes, heart-shaped
  candy boxes, and
  jewelry gift boxes
paint, variety of colors
sponges or sponge
  paintbrushes
glue
sequins and/or stickers

Make Your Great Gift

1. Paint the box lid and sides of the bottom in an up-and-down motion using a sponge. (Overlapping creates colorful surprises!)*
2. After the paint dries, glue on sequins or place stickers on box lid.
3. Place your special gift (see one of the many gifts in this book) in the box to surprise a loved one.

Helpful Hints

- Add a few drops of dish detergent to the paint to help it adhere if you are using boxes with a glossy surface.
- Using paint colors close to that of the box or darker will hide writing and labels on the surface.
- If the bottom section of the box contains writing or pictures, it can be covered with a coat of paint.

Seasonal Suggestions

- Heart-shaped boxes make ideal gift containers for Valentine's Day, Mother's Day, and Father's Day.
- For a winter holiday, paint box top with glue, place lid in zipper-seal sandwich bag with a few tablespoons of glitter, and shake.

* May need adult help or supervision.

Papier-Mâché Gift Box

Have fun transforming a box into a gift box work of art.

Materials

papier-mâché paste
  (see Before Beginning)
newspaper
shoeboxes
bowl(s)
paint
thick paintbrushes

Before Beginning Prepare papier-mâché paste using liquid starch OR equal portions of flour and water OR two parts glue to one part water. Pour chosen paste into a bowl.*

Make Your Great Gift

1. Tear newspaper into strips in various widths and lengths.
2. Dip the newspaper strips one at a time into the papier-mache paste, then slide the strip through two fingers to remove excess paste.
3. Place the strips one at a time on the outer sides of the box, overlapping and filling in spaces.*
4. Allow papier-mâché surface to dry until hard to the touch.
5. Paint the outside of the box using a variety of colors.
6. After the box is dried, place a piece of tissue paper in it and fill with a homemade gift.

Helpful Hints

- Choose one color of paint to brush on as a surface coat. After the paint dries, paint on designs, shapes, and pictures using contrasting colors.
- Gift suggestions to put in the box:
  - weaving band pencil holder (see page 62)
  - stationery (see Chapter 7)
  - bread basket liner and some homemade cookies or bread (see page 83)
  - oatmeal bar cookies, jar, and recipe (see pages 57-60)

* May need adult help or supervision.

Fancy Gift Basket

Jazz up a small gift by presenting it in a basket made from a margarine tub, paint, colored wire, and markers.

Materials

small plastic containers, approximately 8 oz. (clean margarine, sour cream containers)

fine sandpaper, cut in quarters*

paint

non-toxic permanent markers or stickers

paper punch

colored plastic coated wire, approximately 12" piece

Before
Beginning   Wash and dry the plastic container.*

Make Your Great Gift

1. Roughen the sides of the plastic container with a piece of sandpaper. This will help the paint to adhere.
2. Paint the outside of the container, covering the sides completely.
   Optional: After the paint dries, use non-toxic permanent markers to add pictures or designs, or place stickers around the tub on top of the paint.
3. Punch holes on opposite sides of the tub (adult only).
4. Wrap a piece of wire around a pencil to form a "spring." Slide the wire off the pencil.*
5. Push each end of the wire through a hole. Twist to secure. This creates a handle.*
6. Place a piece of tissue paper in the basket, put in a gift, and it is ready.

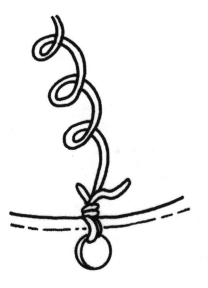

Helpful Hints

■ If lettering on tub shows through paint, cover with another layer or use thicker paint.

■ One option is to sand tubs, and then spray paint them (adult only). Then decorate them with markers and stickers.*

■ Use pipe cleaners instead of plastic-coated wire.

Seasonal Suggestion

■ Provide Easter grass to put in a pastel-colored basket for spring holiday gifts.

Paper Plate Basket

Display homemade gifts in this beautiful basket.

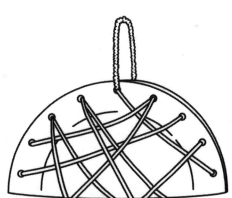

Materials

small paper plate
hole punch
markers
curling ribbon, various
    colors, cut into
      12" lengths*
pipe cleaner

Before Beginning Use the hole punch to make holes about one inch apart all the way around the edge of each paper plate.*

Make Your Great Gift

1. Decorate the paper plate using markers.
2. Weave various colors of curling ribbon through the holes in the plate. When finished, secure the ends of the ribbon with clear tape.*
3. Wrap the ends of a pipe cleaner through holes at opposite ends of the plate to create a handle for the basket.

Helpful Hints

- Decorate the plate with markers and seasonal stickers.
- This basket is great for displaying lightweight homemade cards and gifts. Use it to carry some of the flowers found on pages 28-30.

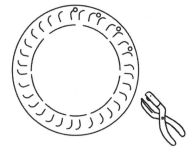

Seasonal Suggestions

- Use pastel markers and ribbon for occasions such as Easter, May Day, and other spring holidays.
- For festive winter holidays such as Christmas, Hanukkah, or New Year's, use foil ribbon and metallic-color crayons in place of plain curling ribbon and markers.

* May need adult help or supervision.

List of Common and Uncommon Holidays

January

1	New Year's Day
13	Anniversary of Frisbee
13	Anniversary of First Radio Broadcast
17	Benjamin Franklin's Birthday
Third Monday in January	Martin Luther King, Jr.'s Birthday
Fourth Wednesday in January	National Compliment Day
Fourth Wednesday in January	National School Nurse Day
Late January-Early February	Chinese New Year

February–Black History Month and Heart Month

2	Groundhog Day
5	Hank Aaron's Birthday
6	Babe Ruth's Birthday
11	Thomas Edison's Birthday
12	Abraham Lincoln's Birthday
14	Valentine's Day
15	Susan B. Anthony's Birthday
Date varies	President's Day
22	Washington's Birthday

March–American Red Cross Month, National Craft Month, and National Women's History Month

2	Dr. Seuss's Birthday
3	Alexander Graham Bells' Birthday
6	Michelangelo's Birthday
17	St. Patrick's Day
21	First Day of Spring
20	National Agriculture Day

April–National Humor Month

1	April Fool's Day
7	World Health Day
16	Moment of Laughter Day
22	Earth Day
Date varies	Easter
Date varies	Passover

May

1	Mother Goose Day
5	Cinco De Mayo
Second Sunday in May	Mother's Day
Last Monday in May	Memorial Day

June–National Candy Month and National Rose Month

14	Flag Day
21	First Day of Summer
Third Sunday in June	Father's Day

July

1	Canada Day
1	Anniversary of First Zoo (Philadelphia)
4	Independence Day
29	Parents' Day

August–National Inventors' Month

6	Sisters' Day
13	Left-Hander's Day

September

First Monday in September	Labor Day
8	International Literacy Day
First Sunday after Labor Day	Grandparents' Day
21	First Day of Fall
Fourth Sunday in September	Good Neighbor Day

October

7	Frugal Fun Day
8	National Children's Day
12	Columbus Day
16	School Librarian Day
24	United Nations' Day
31	Halloween

November

11	Veterans Day
14	National Teddy Bear Day
17	World Peace Day
18	Mickey Mouse's Birthday
20	International Children's Day
Fourth Thursday in November	Thanksgiving

December

6	Saint Nicholas Day
Date varies	Hanukkah
16	Anniversary of Boston Tea Party
21	First Day of Winter
25	Christmas
26	Boxing Day
26-January 1	Kwanzaa
31	New Year's Eve

But don't wait for a holiday or birthday! Making a gift is a great way to...

- Say thank you to grandma for staying with you after school.
- Cheer up a friend who is sick or in the hospital.
- Brighten the day of someone in a nursing home who is feeling sad or lonely.
- Congratulate a sibling for a special accomplishment.
- Send a remembrance to family friends who are moving away.

Make the people you love smile with a gift from the heart!

Materials List

Items that can be collected, saved, and used in the activities

____Aquarium rocks

____Baby food jars

____Beads

____Boxes with lids

____Brown grocery bags

____Bubble packing wrap

____Buttons

____Candy boxes

____Cardboard tubes

____Cardboard

____Cardboard boxes, all types

____Cardboard shirt boxes

____Cellophane scraps

____Check boxes

____Cloth scraps

____Clothespins, spring type

____Colored wire scraps

____Compact discs

____Craft foam pieces

____Crepe paper streamers

____Dried flowers

____Earrings

____Easter grass

____Felt scarps

____Golf balls

____Jewelry gift boxes

____Juice boxes, empty and clean

____Laundry detergent box

____Liquid laundry detergent bottles, with handles

____Marbles

____Margarine lids

____Matte board

____Men's white tube socks

____Packing popcorn

____Paper towel tubes

____Pebbles and stones

____Pizza boxes

____Plastic bottles, 1 liter

____Plastic bottles, 2 liter

____Plastic containers, small with lids

____Potato chip cans

____Quart jars with lids

____Ribbon scraps

____Scarves, with patterns

____Seashells

____Shallow plastic containers

____Shirts, button down, light color

____Shirts, with patterns

____Shoeboxes

____Small plastic flower pots

____Small water bottles

____Stick-on bows

____Styrofoam pieces

____Thread spools

____Three-ring binders

____Ties, with patterns

____Tissue paper

____Toilet paper tubes

____Tube socks

____Wallpaper scraps

____Wood scraps

____Wooden beads

____Wrapping paper scraps

____Wrapping paper tubes

____Yarn scraps

Index

F

Fabric
> felt, 41, 48, 162
> muslin, 56, 110
> paint, 63, 81
> scraps, 40–41, 61, 77, 81, 82, 83, 111, 133

Family activities, 43–60
Father's Day, 16, 19, 59, 69, 71, 78, 83, 88, 118, 131, 133, 135, 154, 160
Feathers, 147
Felt scraps, 41, 48, 162
Film canisters, 138
First Day of Fall, 160
First Day of Spring, 159
First Day of Summer, 160
First Day of Winter, 161
First Zoo Anniversary, 160
Fishing line, 104
Flag Day, 160
Flour, 57–58, 78, 122, 155
Flowerpots, 136
> clay, 38
> homemade, 35
> plastic, 32, 162
> saucers, 84

Flowers, 12, 34, 88, 93, 103, 106, 149
> candy, 29
> dried, 113, 114, 162
> homemade, 28, 37, 151, 158
> photos, 30
> seeds, 33, 35–36
> sticky, 32

Foam. *See also* Craft foam
> balls, 147
> brushes, 31
> sponge, 92

Foil, 14, 17, 29, 84, 113
> aluminum, 118
> confetti, 85, 95, 102, 108

gift wrap, 90, 128, 141, 146
> ribbons, 41, 128, 158
> stickers, 128

Food coloring, 72, 110, 139, 144
Frames, 11–16, 132
> Plexiglas, 15

Franklin, Benjamin birthday, 159
Frugal Fun Day, 161
Fruits, 60
Funnels, 35, 37, 58, 72

G

Games, 46
> I Spy, 45
> Juice Box Memory, 47
> matching, 47
> Pick-Up Sticks, 47
> sorting, 117
> Tick-Tack-Toe, 47
> travel box, 46

Garage sale circle dots, 47
Garden gifts, 33–41
Gemstones, 13, 17, 71, 86, 95, 104, 116
Gift bags, 148–152
Gift baskets, 156–158
Gift boxes, 154–155
Gift wrap, 14, 23, 48, 85, 105, 108, 113, 135, 140–141, 162
> bubble, 144–145
> foil, 90, 128, 141, 146
> footprint, 150–151
> homemade, 143–147
> salty, 146
> sponged, 152
> tape, 148–149
> tubes, 17, 31, 45, 153, 162

Glitter, 118, 124, 146, 154
Glitter crayons, 57, 117

Glitter glue, 15, 48, 77
Glitter paint, 41, 57, 111, 121, 144
Glue, 13–17, 20–22, 24, 29–32, 34, 40, 44–45,
   49–50, 56, 63–64, 66–67, 70–71, 73–74,
   76–77, 82–83, 86, 88–89, 94–95, 98, 100,
   104–105, 108, 112, 114, 118, 124, 128,
   133–135, 138, 140, 146, 153–155
      colored, 84
      defined, 8
      glitter, 15, 48, 77
      guns, 35, 72
      sticks, 35, 87, 96
      watered down, 26
Golf balls, 52, 81, 162
Good Neighbor Day, 160
Grandparents' Day, 16, 37, 44, 62–64, 69, 87,
   109, 160
Gravel, 78
Grocery bags, 86, 148, 152, 162
Groundhog Day, 159

H
Hairspray, 46
Halloween, 118, 161
Hammers
      plastic, 116
Hanukkah, 15, 64, 81, 129, 131, 149, 158, 161
Heart boxes, 154
Heart Month, 159
Hearts, 12, 16, 32, 34, 92–93, 95, 103, 129, 147
Hole punches, 22, 31, 36, 40, 50, 54, 56, 60, 96,
   106, 130, 149, 156, 158
Holidays, 159–160
Honey, 72
Hooks
      screw-in, 100
Hot chocolate mix, 59
Household gifts, 79–98

I
I Spy, 45
Independence Day. *See* July Fourth
Index cards, 30, 56, 59, 133
      unlined, 24, 49, 89, 152
Indian corn, 124
Ink daubers, 86, 96
Ink stamps, 44, 60, 138
Inkpads, 44, 60, 80, 132, 137–138
      metallic color, 138
International Children's Day, 161
International Literacy Day, 160

J
Jars, 155
      baby food, 72, 118, 162
      canning, 57
      plastic, 62
      quart, 56–59, 162
Jellybeans, 85
Jellyroll pans, 145
Jewelry
      boxes, 26, 154, 162
      earrings, 37, 116, 162
      homemade, 74, 77
      jigsaw pins, 124
Jewels. *See* Gemstones
Jingle bells, 113
Juice boxes, 47
Juice can lids, 20, 47, 73
July Fourth, 53, 75, 83, 118, 121, 160

Y